MICKEY**COLEMAN**

G000254598

PULSE

A MEMOIR ON LIFE, NEAR-DEATH, AND A NEW LIFE

With Damian Harvey

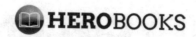

PUBLISHED BY HERO BOOKS
LUCAN
CO. DUBLIN
IRELAND

Hero Books is an imprint of Umbrella Publishing
First Published 2023

ISBN: 9781910827857

A CIP record for this book is available from the British Library

Cover design and formatting: jessica@viitaladesign.com
Photographs: The Coleman Family Collection, and Sportsfile

DEDICATION

*To my wife Erin who lifted me up
when I couldn't walk.*

*To my father, Sean and mother, Teresa
who have shaped me into the man I am today.
I am forever grateful.*

CO-AUTHOR

DAMIAN HARVEY is a close friend of Mickey Coleman. They met while forming the New York branch of Club Tyrone, the preeminent fundraising arm of Tyrone GAA. This is Damian's first foray into the world of ghost writing an autobiography but it's unlikely to be his last. He is a member of the Teamtalkmag media team based in County Tyrone.

Contents

Prologue

Epilogue

Foreword

September 1993, the setting is a classroom in Holy Trinity College, Cookstown.

It's my first year out as a qualified PE teacher, and as a new recruit, my timetable requires me to teach Religion.

I've gotten the heads up from a few of my teaching colleagues that they wouldn't be exactly queuing up to teach this particular group of Fifth Years.

The reason why soon became very obvious. It wasn't helped by the fact that they were not really interested in the intricacies of various religious denominations that happened to be on the curriculum.

It's only a few days in, when I ask the class to take out their homework from the night before. A hand goes up at the back of the class and the conversation goes something like this:

'I've no homework done, sir.'

'Why not?'

'Holy ghost boys, how will me knowing anything about the Greek Orthodox Church put any spuds on my table?'

'Right, what's your name?'

'Mickey Coleman!'

'Ok Mickey, stay behind, and I'll talk to you after class.'

He did stay behind, and I did have a conversation with him... the first of many!!

Exactly 10 years on from our introduction and many 'holy ghosts' later, Mickey and myself were among the first group of men from Tyrone to climb the steps of the Hogan Stand in Croke Park to lift the ultimate prize in Irish sport, the Sam Maguire Cup.

A high fielder and fierce competitor on the field of play, Mickey was often the centre of attention off it, with his sharp wit, storytelling and choice of song captivating many an audience on memorable nights out.

How he managed to convince the 2003 team to agree to release a song *Total Faith* before the All-Ireland final is beyond me and speaks volumes for his persuasive powers. In terms of his songwriting, it is a ballad that he never wanted to pen that is perhaps his most powerful... *The Brantry Boy*.

This song, a fitting tribute to a Cormac, who was our friend and teammate. It captured the mood and sombre feelings in a shocked county so eloquently. Mickey did a fantastic job on it.

A man with drive and ambition, it was no surprise that Mickey headed west. New York it appeared welcomed him with open arms and in a short space of time connections were made and business began to flourish.

Be it music, football or work, Mickey was top of his game and in meeting Erin, the love of his life, he had eventually met someone that could put manners on him.

With things going well, Mickey made frequent trips home to support his club Ardboe, Holy Trinity College in their new build project and, of course, the county that he played for. He's as passionate about his club and county as any other man I know. He's not afraid to put his hand in his own pocket and encourage others in New York to do the same in order to support Tyrone.

He was enjoying life to the full when it all came crashing down on the 29th March 2021.

This book will take you to Mickey's darkest hour and, from there, onwards to his remarkable journey of recovery.

They say it's a hard to keep a good man down... and from him finding a way to put spuds on the table.

Enjoy!

Peter Canavan
September 2023

Acknowledgements

I WOULD LIKE to express my sincere gratitude to Damian Harvey for his hard work in bringing my story to life. Countless hours of conversations, a few transatlantic flights, and a lot of tea and coffee has really bonded a great friendship with myself and Damian. The crafting of this book has made us laugh and cry, but most of all, it has been therapeutic. Thank you, Damian, for pushing me to get this done. I will be forever grateful.

To my father, Sean, mother, Teresa, brothers, Shane, Raymond and Ryan, and sisters, Andrea, Sharon, Gemma, and Clodagh, who have always supported me through the years, thank you for that support. We were never the Irish family for hugs or kisses or expressing our feelings through the years but, in many ways, you have always shown me your love. That is something I hold dear and we have a loving bond that will never be broken.

To my wife, Erin's family. Grandparents, Mike and Peggy, parents, Frankie and Kitty, and John and Margie, sisters, Blaithin and Neidín, and brother, John Paul, you have always looked after me and took me under your wing and made my life in America a pleasant one. In my darkest days you were always there with kindness and love. Thank you from the bottom of my heart.

To the Orangetown police department, the Pearl River Ambulance service, the team of surgeons, doctors, nurses, the cardiac rehab center, and the entire staff at Montefiore Nyack Hospital, thank you all for saving my life. I particularly want to thank a young man, Thomas Suffern, who administered CPR on me for six and a half minutes against all odds. I am indebted to you for your determination and desire to keep me alive. Thank you.

To a special man and friend whom I've known for almost 10 years, Fr Brendan Fitzgerald, a Kerry man and the pastor of Barnabas parish in the Woodlawn section of the Bronx, New York. You have been a spiritual mentor to me, thank you.

To all my family and friends, and everyone from all over the world who sent well wishes and prayers, your energy played a huge part in my recovery.

To all the people who have impacted my life through the years; my schoolteachers, business partners, musicians, football coaches and all the great teams that I have had the privilege to be a part of. One special team that I had the honor to play on was my native home team of Ardboe. I was very fortunate to win a county title in 1998 with this group of men whom I grew up with. Ardboe and its people will always have a special place in my heart.

My two incredible sons, Micheal and Riordan, someday you will read this and fully understand how much I love you both. You are so precious to me, and you fill me with love every day. I love you to the moon and back.

My amazing wife, Erin, you have been my guiding light for these past 11 years. You have been by my side through it all. No words will ever do justice to how much I love you and how much I appreciate everything you have done for me, especially in the past two years.

You have been my strength and courage. You are a beautiful human being, and I am forever grateful to have you as my wife. I look forward to many more years together playing our music. I love you.

Thank you for our amazing family.

Mickey Coleman
September 2023

PROLOGUE

Stay Alive

Every man has two lives, and the second starts
when he realises, he has just one.

(Confucius)

MARCH 29, 2021.

IN MY LIFE, I have a lot to be thankful for.

A beautiful wife.

Two great children.

Money in the bank.

A thriving business.

Behind me, a sporting career that yielded something good, and the promise of more.

I AM 41 years of age and have started taking my training seriously. I am just after running 5 kilometres in 19 minutes and 45 seconds. That's just over six-minute mile pace.

I feel like I'm flying.

Only, I'm flying alright. In some spacy sub-consciousness in my own armchair.

Because I am dying.

I am slipping away. The dark is on the fringes of my sight, and it is inching closer to the centre.

My hearing is failing. My strength ebbing.

My chest is caving in, and I am fainting… and I need to stop it.

SO, I THUMP my chest.

Hard as I can… to try to do something. I know that it is my heart. I only leaned forward to set a cup of tea on a foot-stool… and it hit me.

I get to the bottom of the stairs. Upstairs is Erin… my wife. My children.

The stairs are like a cliff face. I cannot get up there. I must get up there.

Up there is help. I shout for Erin… Nothing comes out.

I get to the top of the stairs. I push the door open… and fall through it.

'I'm going out,' I say to Erin as she makes the calls.

I KNEW I was in the fight of my life.

I was banging my chest with my right fist. Banging it as hard as I could… performing my own CPR. In my mind, something was blocked in my heart, and I needed to get something moved in it.

Like a mantra, I keep saying the same things to myself…

Inaudible to others… *You've got to stay strong.*

You've got to stay strong. *Stay Alive… Stay Alive.*

Stay Alive. It made no difference.

I was getting weaker by the second. Another punch to the chest and the overwhelming pain. I was fighting tooth and nail to keep going.

To keep oxygen in my body. With every step I took going down those stairs, I felt like I was lowering myself down into a dark hole in the ground.

At the bottom step, I sank to one knee.

Two Orangetown police officers made their way inside the front door. I reached out my hand…

'Lads… can somebody help me.'

On the word 'me'… everything went hazy, and the light left my eyes.

MY NAME IS Mickey Coleman.

I have it all and I have nothing. What once was, is gone.

Second chances are few and far between.

I'm living the second chance.

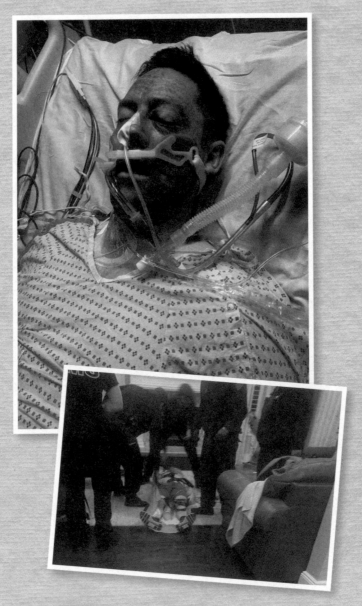

Mickey Coleman lies in a coma in Montefoire Nyack Hospital (above) after collapsing in his Pearl River home in March of 2021. He lies on the floor being attended to by medical personnel and police officers.

PART 1

That Day

IT'S FUNNY THE tricks that the brain plays with memory. Piecing it all together now is still a challenging task.

There are gaps... that I can't quite fill.

There are gaps that I know that I probably will never be able to fill, and then there are parts of it all that flood back into my mind with great clarity.

That happens at times when I least expect it.

That Monday was a day set apart from any other Monday. That Monday would redefine who I am and give me a perspective on things that very few people will ever experience.

Talk to those who know me.

They will tell you that I'm not shy when it comes to talking. I've always been able to tell a story. Lots of those stories include a sizeable portion of near-truths and half-truths.

Let me assure you that what happened to me on Monday, March 29, 2021 was no near-truth or half-truth. It rocked my very foundations and has changed my outlook on life forever.

That day has both haunted and inspired me in equal measures.

And it continues to do so.

I'VE ALWAYS SAID that there are two types of Irishmen that land in America.

They left Ireland with the same dream of making it big in the United States. First, you've got the guy who reckons that as long as you can find a gaelic football club, and that you will make it as a star player, then you can pretty much start every day at any time you want.

The second type of Irishman knows that unless you are prepared to get out of your bed early, then by 9am, most days around New York City feel like lunchtime.

Those in the first category don't last too long in this city. They get themselves attached to a GAA club somewhere and if they are lucky, they might even make a few dollars playing here during the summer.

I learned quickly that if you want to survive in this city, that you need to think sharp, act sharp... and move sharp.

Yes, you can play all the gaelic football you want, but you need to be prepared to work your ass off every day, or your stay will be short lived. You simply won't be able to pay for your rent and have a decent lifestyle.

BY MARCH 2021, my company, Shoreline Builders Inc, was going well.

I had built it up from scratch and it was growing at a rate that I could still handle. As with most other Monday mornings, I liked to get out on the job sites.

That day, I met up with another Irishman, my Director of Operations Derek Barry at the Shoreline office in midtown Manhattan.

We grabbed a coffee, hit the subway, and jumped on the number 7 train to Long Island City. We had a drywall fitout project going on there at the time.

I remember meeting the guys on the job site. They were pouring concrete on a roof deck. It was a sizeable job and it took some time to walk the site and talk through some of the issues that had arisen.

I don't recall much of what happened the rest of that working day, but I do remember grabbing lunch at a diner nearby my office.

The only other outstanding work-related memory that I have from that day is a difficult one for me to explain. Truth be told I can't explain it. One of the guys in the office confirmed this in the aftermath of everything.

I got up from my desk.

I walked out of my own office and made my way across the Shoreline floorspace to the elevator.

I pinged the elevator.

Entered it and, for some reason unknown to me, spoke to no one before I left.

What the hell was I thinking about?

That wasn't me. It simply wasn't me.

It didn't matter what kind of a mood I was in. Normally, I'd make a point of saying goodbye to people before I left the office.

For some reason that day, I didn't do that.

I've thought a lot about that action since I've recovered. Was there a reason, sub-consciously, that I chose to do that? What if that had been my last visit to the office?

It almost was.

That wasn't me.

The drive home that day is another blank space in my mind, but a well-worn one too.

The car was always parked in the garage opposite Shoreline Builders on 36th Street.

A quick turn right had me on 5th Avenue, and another right turn brought me along 34th Street, right the way across to 9A which hugged the Hudson River. I'd follow 9A right the way up to the slipway for the George Washington Bridge.

Once I crossed that, I'd swing the car onto the Palisades Interstate Parkway, which in turn brought me all the way into Orangeburg.

The final section of the journey is the short drive along Veterans Memorial Drive, and into Gilbert Avenue in Peal River.

What if it had happened when I was driving home from work?

Pearl River, Orangetown, Rockland County, New York, had been my home for the previous two years.

I do remember speaking to Erin when I got home.

Erin needed to visit one of the restaurants in Pearl River. She was tasked with arranging her grandmother's 80th birthday party and needed to get something booked in.

Before she left the house, Erin put the two kids to bed. It was just me and the two boys.

What if had happened when it was just me and the two boys in the house?

The potential impact of that is only hitting me now.

It's sending shivers up my spine.

I got lucky.

ERIN RETURNED TO the house about 7:30pm.

By that time, I was out of my work clothes and into my maroon CrossFit shorts, grey t-shirt and runners, and I was ready to hit the road for a run.

We found out that Erin was pregnant with our second child in January, 2018. It was Micháel's third birthday, and it was a lovely present for us all. As a couple we had our date nights and our dinners out, and we normally had a glass or two of wine.

As Erin wasn't going to be able to take alcohol during her pregnancy and I wanted to make some kind of sacrifice to support her during that time, I decided that I wouldn't drink either. I also made a promise to her that I was going to go back and train, and take my physical health a bit more seriously.

I'D COME FROM a background of playing gaelic football in Ireland, and for the best part of my life training hard was something that I was used to. After a few years away from a higher level of physical fitness, I decided that the time was right to commit to something that was going to challenge me. I needed that challenge.

I didn't want to just be going out doing my own thing. The odd run and going through the motions wasn't going to cut it for me.

In early 2018, I spent some time doing my homework on some local CrossFit gyms. Following on from that bit of research, I ended up joining North East CrossFit gym in Eastchester, New York. It was just 15 minutes from home in Pearl River.

Close enough to get there quickly, and far enough away from home that meant

I didn't know any of the other members there.

I clearly remember the first day that I went in there.

It was 5am.

It was snowing outside and while that left things a little tricky, what happened inside was on another level of uncomfortable. It was brutal. They were some of the toughest physical fitness sessions I ever engaged in.

What am I doing here?

Why am I even bothering with this?

Those were my constant thoughts that first morning.

GROWING UP PLAYING gaelic football was something that I was always comfortable with. It was easy. It was familiar. You never felt out of your comfort zone. I always believed I could compete with the best players in the club, and with most of the best players in the county.

The first day that I walked into that North East CrossFit gym, I felt like a first grader walking into a new school for the first time.

I was way outside my comfort zone.

I could do little or nothing in those early sessions. I couldn't even squat properly. I'd little or no flexibility. People were laughing with me, when I attempted to engage in some of the stretching.

After some sensible advice from the instructors, I spent the first four weeks concentrating mainly on the mobility classes that the gym offered. Even then it was tough, and it was brutal. There were occasions when I wasn't sure that I was going to be able to walk back to the car after a session.

The only reason I survived was because the people there were such a positive bunch. They accepted me into their group. They encouraged me through every single session.

The early pain quickly turned to energy, and I soon became addicted to it.

Erin gave birth to our second son, Riordan on August 31, 2018. He was born on the Friday, and Tyrone, my native county, were due to play Dublin in the All-Ireland gaelic football final two days later.

All-Ireland finals are the pinnacle for gaelic footballers in Ireland and as a former county footballer myself, I was keeping close attention as to how Tyrone were doing throughout that season.

At one point I thought about catching a flight to Dublin for the game.

It was more than a thought. I'd checked flight availability, hotel accommodation in Dublin, schedules, and prices. It wasn't something that I'd shared with Erin, as I figured out that leaving my wife and my new son to fly over to Ireland wasn't a smart idea. The truth was that I knew my immediate health and well-being would have been under threat from a risk that I eventually thought the better of taking.

For the next three years, I kept the CrossFit going and I found that running complimented it. Running after work in the evenings had come first, but CrossFit got me running in a way that was much better than I ever ran before.

At 41 years of age, I was in the shape of my life. I was physically feeling better than I had at any previous point in my life.

The evening running route never changed.

After a short time, it became very familiar to me. I'd run it on autopilot. The stopwatch was started, as I stepped off the front porch as per normal.

THE FIRST 30 yards took me to the end of my driveway.

Then I turned right through the gates, and onto Washington Avenue.

A few yards later, I'd cross the street.

Make a right turn down North Henry Street.

Onwards towards Middletown Road.

It was all footpath, or sidewalk as they call it in this part of the world. It was safe and uncomplicated. That first part of the run was all downhill. A chance to regulate my breathing. It was a great way to stretch out the legs and loosen up at the beginning of the route. Everything was measured.

I'd always monitor my progress on the watch against the various landmarks, which for me were marked by various fire hydrants along the route.

Those fire hydrants were my benchmarks.

A quick glance at the watch gave me the feedback that I needed. Long before stopping the watch at the end of the run, I'd know exactly how I was going.

That night I must have been flying along the route.

The challenging part of the run always started along Gilbert Avenue.

A long… slow uphill stretch that looped back in towards the centre of Pearl River.

Gilbert Avenue is a peaceful part of the world at that time of the evening. It was on the suburbs of the town, and quiet. Sometimes you'd meet four or five cars on that stretch of road at that time of the evening. Sometimes none.

What if it had happened there?

As the run edged closer to the town of Pearl River, the route levelled out somewhat.

The next part took me towards the Post Office and the Chase Bank at the traffic lights.

The final section was a gradual rise uphill and back towards Washington Avenue.

A couple of hundred yards later, I'd be back at bottom of my driveway again. And home.

That last section provided a stiff challenge.

Nonetheless it was one that I looked forward to because I knew that the run was almost over. I was close to home.

EVERY RUN ENDED with the button on the stopwatch being hit as I reached the steps of the porch in front of the house. Afterwards, I followed the run up with a few stretches.

The steps of the porch provided a good platform for those exercises.

Before I went back into the house, I'd take a few minutes to reset my breathing normally by taking a seat on the top step of the porch. That was always the routine.

It was the same every single time.

Sitting there, feeling tired and strong.

Sitting on my porch.

Feeling rich in health.

Thinking.

Waiting momentarily, before going inside to say, 'I'm back' to my wife.

Sitting there, those precious few minutes, my breathing almost settled back down, thinking… about everything… and nothing.

And, more than anything, feeling enriched by my run.

By my life.

Thinking about my old home, maybe.

Thinking about my new home.

Thinking about my working life.

Calm thoughts.

Strong thoughts.

Feeling peaceful and in charge of my life.

Then… suddenly, for no good reason, I'd be on my feet and opening the front door.

I CANNOT REMEMBER a single thing about the run that day. All I have as a permanent marker from the run is a stopwatch that was on my wrist that day.

It still has the time on it.

19 minutes 45 seconds.

Fifteen seconds faster than I'd ever run that route before. What an achievement. The crazy thing is I don't even remember how I felt when I saw it.

19 minutes 45 seconds.

What happened next is a mixture of things that I remember and other parts that Erin has helped me piece together. Erin made me a sandwich, and a cup of Barry's decaffeinated tea, before she made her way up the stairs to our bedroom.

Our home in Pearl River is never without a box of Barry's tea. A little bit of Ireland that I'm quite sure forms a part of many Irish American homes.

I took a seat in the armchair in the living room and switched on the TV to catch up with the news on RTÉ. I reached over to set the mug of tea on the footstool and, as I sat back in the chair… it happened.

BANG!

It hit me.

Jesus Christ! What the hell is happening me?

The unmerciful pain almost shut me down immediately.

It was as if my chest caved in.

I felt like I was fainting.

Almost immediately, I started thumping my chest with my fist to see if I could clear it. *Surely a good thump of my chest with my fist will clear whatever the hell is causing this?*

It was a pain that I'd never experienced before.

I knew that this was serious, and I knew it was my heart. When it happens, believe me you know exactly what it is. I knew immediately that I had limited time to get help.

I was in trouble.

Deep trouble.

I GATHERED UP every morsel of strength that I could and stumbled to the bottom of the stairs. The breath almost left me again as another strike of pain screamed across my lungs and chest.

How am I going to survive this?

I was gripped by fear.

When I turned the corner to look up the steps, it felt like I was staring up the face of a cliff. Somehow, I managed to negotiate the first few steps.

I tried to shout for Erin, but I couldn't get the words that I needed to say out of my mouth.

BANG!

Another bolt of lightning hit me.

It arrived like a shockwave seizing up every tissue sinew in my chest. Then… the pain. An unmerciful pain.

I'm not sure how but I scrambled up the remaining steps and eventually made it to the door of our bedroom. As I opened it, I managed to get the words out of my mouth.

'Erin, please… help me.

'I think I'm taking a heart attack.'

She jumped up out of bed.

'Mickey you've obviously gone too hard in the run.'

Her voice was calm.

'You've over-pushed yourself.'

18 minutes 45 seconds.

Had those 15 seconds off my best time cost me everything?

I'd no time to contemplate anything… I needed to… breathe.

Please… give me another clear breath.

Erin called 911.

ANOTHER LIGHTNING BOLT.

More excruciating pain.

Seconds later, she had a cold towel around my neck as I slumped onto one knee in the en suite.

Suddenly, for the first time since the first strike… the pain subsided.

I turned to Erin and told her that the pain had gone.

'It's better… it's better!'

Less than ten seconds later… another huge strike.

This time much worse than before.

I was completely overcome by it.

MY MIND WAS in turmoil.

I'm dying.

Jesus Christ, I'm going to die.

I spluttered out some words to Erin.

'I'm going out!'

I could see the anguish in her face. She needed to find a way to help me. She encouraged me to try and make it back down the stairs.

Somehow, I found the energy once again to get to the top of the stairs. As I attempted to ease myself down the stairs, the pain rolled in once again.

Is this it?

Is this how it's going to end for me?

Has my time come?

PULSE

I WAS IN the fight of my life.
Every single breath.
Every half-breath was so important.
I kept on banging my chest with my right fist.
Thumping that fist into my chest...
As hard as I could.
It was as if I was performing my own CPR.

IN MY MIND, something was blocked in my heart. I needed to get something moved in it. Another fist thumped into my chest.

I kept uttering words to myself... 'You got to stay strong... You got to stay strong!'

'Stay Alive

'Stay Alive.

'STAY ALIVE!'

IT MADE NO difference.

I could feel myself getting weaker by the second. Another punch to the chest.

In my mind, I thought that this would keep the blood flowing to my heart. The truth was the pain was overwhelming. I was fighting tooth and nail... to keep going. To keep oxygen in my body.

With every step I took going down those stairs... I was lowering myself down into that dark hole.

I clambered over the last step.

Sank to one knee.

Seconds later, the two Orangetown officers made their way inside the front door. I reached out my hand.

'Lads... can somebody help me!'

As I uttered the last syllable everything went hazy...

Darkness.

THE WIDOW-MAKER HAD knocked on my door.

I'd walked straight into it.

PART **2**
Ardboe

LET ME INTRODUCE you to Ardboe.

It's a small rural community on the western shores of Lough Neagh in County Tyrone. Slap bang in the middle of the North of Ireland.

It's a place like hundreds of other rural communities around the island of Ireland. Life when I was growing up revolved around two things. Gaelic football and mass on a Sunday. Those were the two constants.

Beside Ardboe is Lough Neagh. Back in my childhood it provided lots of employment opportunities for the fishermen that worked it at all hours of the day and night.

New York and the United States in particular had very close links to our community. During the Second World War the United States Air Force took over the airfield base in Ardboe and brought over three and a half thousand military personnel to the area. The remnants of that airfield are operational, but the military aeroplanes are now replaced by lorries, vans and trucks moving goods and machinery from what is now a business park.

The 39 houses of Lakeview Cottages were known to us and many others as 'The Little Bronx'. It was a stone's throw from Ardboe airfield. Those houses and the surrounding area formed the centre of our universe.

MONEY MIGHT WELL have been hard to come by, but we were millionaires when it came to the wealth that a fiercely loyal and close community offers. Everyone looked out for each other. In Ardboe, when someone is in need, the whole community pulls in around them.

My father, Sean and mother, Teresa had eight children.

brothers, Shane, Raymond and Ryan, and there were four girls in
Irea, Sharon, Gemma and Clodagh.
xtremes in our house.

Daddy never had much to say. He kept himself to himself. The expression on
his face always spoke more than a thousand words. Those facial expressions told
us exactly how he felt. We became experts at reading his face.

Mummy on the other hand had plenty to say. She was, indisputably, 'The
Boss'.

In the case of an indiscretion, she would attempt to slap you with something,
anything, that was close to her hand. My ability to move quickly meant she rarely
met her target.

Work for mummy included time in the local fish factory. Her real job was
running our house. She was the glue that kept everything together. The one
person, no matter what was going on, that made sure things ran smoothly.

With eight children in such a small home, things were a little crazy at times.
We may have lacked space and the luxuries of a big modern day home, but I can
safely say that I had a brilliant childhood in that house.

There is an incredible power that comes with knowing that both your parents
loved you to bits. That was returned to both of them by all of us. That was our
world inside the four walls of that house in Lakeview Cottages. The beautiful
simplicity of an Irish family, and everything that goes with it. Laughter and tears.
Music, banter and at times tough challenges met and negotiated.

Outside the home was different. It was mayhem.

OUTSIDE, WERE THE dangers of a society that had dragged itself down into
a dark place.

Growing up in the 1980s in Ardboe meant growing up in an environment
dominated by The Troubles. The North was a canvass of shootings, bombings,
hunger strikes, sectarianism, and murder. It was a hellish existence.

Ardboe witnessed many shootings and it crawled with British Army activity.
Rarely a month went by that we didn't get a visit from the British soldiers to the
house. Sometimes it was accompanied with a knock on the door first.

More often than not, it wasn't. The sight of a fully armed British soldier
crashing through your front door is certainly something that grabs your attention.

Back then we had an Alsatian dog at the house. It didn't last too long.

The British Army poisoned it. As far as they were concerned, that dog denied them the element of the surprise.

Daddy was taken away by the Brits on several occasions. Detention, with or without a charge, for men in and around East Tyrone wasn't uncommon during those times. That meant regular prison visits. They were far from easy.

Our father wasn't the only man from our part of County Tyrone that ended up in a jail. Republicans in the North of Ireland support an end to British rule. That meant life dealing with the threat of intimidation and the force of the justice system… British-style.

Visits to Crumlin Road Prison in Belfast terrified me.

THE FIRST THING that grabbed your attention was the smell of damp.

Then the noise.

The slamming of heavily fortified doors.

The rattling of keys inside the locks.

The voices and shouts of the men on the wings of the prison.

I detested being there, but I knew that I had to be there for daddy.

I have no idea what he thought or how he felt about his time in there. It was never discussed at home.

Outwardly, he treated it as if it never happened.

THE TROUBLES RUMBLED on around me for most of my teenage years. Sometimes very far from Ardboe. Sometimes… right on our doorstep.

On July 13, 1984, local members of the Irish Republican Army planned and attempted to carry out an incendiary attack on a local factory to mark the anniversary of the death of one of the Irish Republican hunger strikers, Martin Hurson.

Willie Price was part of the group.

The British Army SAS were lying in wait for him and three other members of the IRA. When they got close to the bushes alongside the factory, the SAS emerged, and all hell broke loose.

Willie was shot dead.

The whole incident occurred just a matter of yards from the rear of our house. From the vantage point of my second-floor bedroom window, I was able to see the aftermath of everything that had happened.

The Little Bronx was saturated by the British army and the Royal Ulster

Constabulary for days after that. The entire housing estate locked down for the duration.

The undercover soldiers that shot Willie celebrated that killing with whoops of cheers. Later it would be confirmed that they produced a cake in their barracks, in the shape of a cross. Willie's name with RIP marked on it.

In the weeks and months that followed, cars were stopped on numerous occasions by the Brits. Shopping and personal belongings often strewn across the road before people were inevitably let go about their business.

It was normal.

For us, it was normal.

Their authority was oppressive and reached everywhere. Even out on Lough Neagh they had their own British army boat, patrolling around the place and hassling local fishermen.

The response from the locals was to show no fear of them whatsoever.

People worked around them.

That was Ardboe in the 1980s and early 90s. The vast majority of people in and around Ardboe felt that the British army shouldn't have been in our part of Ireland.

We were always very proud of the fact that we were Irish. I've always been proud of the fact that I'm an Irish Republican. That is who I am.

I'm proud of my identity.

I want to see the north of Ireland freed from British rule. It was only after the ceasefire and the signing of the Good Friday Agreement that you actually realised the shit show that we all had been living in.

How we all got through it, I will never know.

As children, we dealt with it in a similar way. We went on being kids.

WE SPENT MOST of our spare time out on the big grass green area in front of our home playing football until it was dark.

It wasn't the only football that captured our attention. As the major sports and tournaments rolled on and off our television screens, the sporting calendar in Lakeview Cottage changed too.

Sometimes we were the best soccer players in the world.

Sometimes we were serving for the Wimbledon title over a makeshift tennis net.

Football, and by 'football' I mean gaelic football or Irish football as a lot of friends in the United States call, was the major sport in my life. Gaelic football, from as far back as I can remember, defined my sporting life.

My earliest memory of the game was sitting as a substitute on the bench for an Ardboe under-12 team. I was eight years old at the time. There were no big bags of money in our house, but mummy and daddy did everything they could to make things work for us, best illustrated by my first set of football boots which were ordered from the 'club book'.

Mummy ordered them and paid them off in instalments.

I couldn't believe it when they arrived in the mail. Before that I'd been borrowing boots but, now… I had my own. A set of black football boots with the title 'World Cup' emblazoned in white on the side of each of them.

I think I spent most of the first day staring at them and admiring them. It wasn't long until I had them worn off me. It mattered not that I was playing on grass or tarmac. The boots stayed on. I played away.

I wore them until there wasn't a stud to be seen on them.

The local GAA pitch was where we turned dreams of playing for Ardboe into reality. During the summer we would play there every day. At the weekends, we would pull on the club jersey and play in competitive underage competitions.

I was fortunate to play on a range of successful underage teams with Ardboe. The games with Ardboe were competitive and enjoyable, but what happened on the green outside our house brought competitiveness to a completely different level. Survive those game and you could survive anywhere.

It was brutal at times.

There wasn't a referee in sight. That's because no referee would ever have been able to handle it. My brother, Shane sorted out the really nasty disputes. He was two years older than me. I idolised him. We were best friends, almost like twins.

We kept going. Through it all.

We were living in a kind of hell in our part of Ireland during that time.

But it felt like Heaven.

When the Cuckoo is calling
O're woodland and valley
And the tern and the swallow
They fly O're our bay
Then it's longing I'll be
For the land of my father
Where Bann and Blackwater
Sweep down to Lough Neagh

A home I have made
This land of the stranger
It's many long years
Since I left Derry Quay
Still, I dream of the bloom
And the glens of old Ireland
Where Bann and Blackwater
Sweep down to Lough Neagh

(*The Tern and the Swallow* recorded on Mickey Coleman's album, *Last Glance*)

WORK FOR DADDY meant fishing.

He would make his way down to Lough Neagh shore and out onto the water in a small boat, alongside his brother-in-law, Peter Kelly.

Daddy fished alongside Peter, until Peter passed away from cancer in 1995.

The boat was 28-feet long with a small cabin to the front of it. A big diesel engine drowned out most of the conversation. The boat would be packed with fishing nets and barrels for the nets. There wasn't much room to move around it.

Sometimes, I joined Daddy and Peter, and his son, Peter James, who was the same age as me. The main catch during the summer months was eels.

There wasn't much work to be got out of Peter James or myself at the start. Those days didn't last long. Peter and daddy didn't like the idea of two freeloaders along for the ride. We were expected to get our hands dirty and get stuck in. That's exactly what happened. Fishing on Lough Neagh isn't for the fainthearted. Hauling up a 56-pound anchor and pulling fish out of nets with waves washing up over the top of the boat was dangerous work. The eel season, out on Lough Neagh ran from May to September. When the summer months gave way, the boat would then fish for pollan or grunt fish. It was tough work.

There is nothing glamorous about making your way down to an old shed beside the lough shore for an evening of picking fish out of nets. Even on a summer evening, it was cold and wet. Most of all… the smell was awful.

Picture fish bursting in your hand and you trying to squeeze them out of a net. It used to make me feel nauseous. There was no word of going home until the fish were boxed up for the market and the nets prepped and hauled onto the boat, ready to be reset the next day.

I hated the cold nights from September through to November. That was what we had to do.

It was that simple. There wasn't a choice other than to just get on with it.

As a teenager, I fished with Ned Sheehy, who was another cousin of ours. We did a couple of seasons fishing pollan. It didn't take me too long to realise that it wasn't something that I wanted as a career path.

Daddy and Peter fished for eels for well over 20 years. When Peter passed away the boat was removed from the water, and it was never placed back in it. Things like that happened. Fishing was a generational thing. When a generation passed on, sometimes the boat was retired too.

Daddy fished in other boats for a year or two after that, but his heart was never really in it. That companionship that he had built up with Peter was gone, and with Peter's passing went a major part of daddy's working life.

PULSE

THERE WERE NO lifejackets.

Sometimes, however, there was fear.

Daddy never showed any fear.

And I couldn't show him any fear. I made sure not to look into his eyes... or have him look deep into mine.

But, daddy was too busy anyhow... to see me for long.

That was the secret.

Stay busy... forget the fear, forget the smell... the guts.

Forget the swell.

Balance, and work and work... and work.

Forget the damp, the wetness.

Forget the water altogether... if I can?

I WAS EDUCATED at St Patrick's Primary School in Mullinahoe, Ardboe. I wasn't long at school when the principal, Master McGranaghan, was replaced by Bertie Foley from Dungannon. He was a huge influence on our early gaelic football development.

Bertie saw the value of football and he skilfully used it as a carrot on the end of a stick when he wanted us to behave in class and get stuck into the books.

We lived for the football training sessions that he oversaw. Those sessions would result in four players from the school representing Ardboe in Tyrone's first All-Ireland winning team in 2003.

Frank McGuigan Jnr, his brother Brian McGuigan, Gavin 'Horse' Devlin and I would all be there in Croke Park on that historic day for the county.

Bertie Foley was the driving force behind all of that.

After Primary school, I only ever wanted to go to post-primary school in Cookstown. At 11 years old I transferred to St Patrick's High School in Cookstown in September 1990.

St Patrick's High School was a very different place to the Holy Trinity College that occupies the same building today. At that time, it was an all-boys school. The Troubles were in full flow and education for us wasn't even close to what was important in our lives. My attendance at school was sporadic.

More often, than not, I'd skip school and take a day off to go out on the lough to fish with my father. Sometimes I'd take time off to go and gather potatoes for local farmers. Any additional money that we made at that went straight into the house.

One day I left the house in my uniform and school bag on my back and ended up on Lough Neagh with my father, fishing. I made the mistake of leaving the school bag on the boat that evening, and going into school the next day without it.

I was sent immediately to the vice-principal's office. Donal Campbell was the VP of St Patrick's High School back then. Donal lived in Ardboe and, luckily for me, had a leaning towards Ardboe students in the school.

'Mickey where is the school bag?'

'Sir, to be honest with you... I left it in the head of the boat yesterday when I was out fishing.' He just laughed. Donal knew the craic. He was a good man. I had no time for the schoolbooks at all. My focus was on making the school gaelic football team. That meant sticking close to the teachers who were managing the team and trying to keep in their good books. I was able to master that.

Master 'Cookie' McGuckin made me captain of the school football team for three years in-a-row. Himself and Master Kennedy looked after the school team and football soon became the only thing that kept me interested in school.

By September 1993, I had reached Year 11 and things were about to significantly change in our school world.

A decision had been taken to amalgamate St Patrick's and St Mary's Girls' High School. The new school was to be known as Holy Trinity College Cookstown. Same building under a different banner.

It was a real transition period for students and teachers alike, and it brought about a set of circumstances that formed the foundation for everything that I was about to become.

As in many cases, school amalgamations bring with them a turnover of staff. Some St Patrick's and St Mary's teachers saw this as their opportunity to retire and move out. The Holy Trinity amalgamation brought in a surge of new teachers into the school. Including a guy called Peter Canavan.

AS MOST PEOPLE already know, Peter would go on to make a name for himself as one of the best gaelic footballers ever to play the game.

The Messi of Ireland. The LeBron James of gaelic football and County Tyrone.

Peter might be as famous as LeBron in Ireland, but the only time he reached 6' 9" was when he was standing on the fifth step of a set of stairs. Peter Canavan had hair. Messi also has hair that only Peter can dream of.

As a new teaching recruit to Holy Trinity, Peter was already well known to us. As a Tyrone minor and under-21 player, he was making the headlines. Ulster titles at both those grades and an All-Ireland title at under-21 made him one of the rising stars of the game. Everyone knew him.

We knew all the players on the Tyrone senior team. Most kids around that age are obsessed with gaelic football. We all knew who Peter Canavan was; by the time he began his first teaching post in our school he was firmly established on the Tyrone senior team. We only thought that we *knew* him.

Out on the field he was a classy player, but he had the odd ruthless streak in him. Inside the school, he was totally ruthless. Direct and always to the point.

In those early days he and I didn't get on at all. Every new teacher needed testing out and there wasn't a better bunch of lunatics than us to look for gaps in their temperament. We knew all the right buttons to push. We needed to find out where their boundaries were. We had success with some of the new teachers.

Not with Canavan. Canavan was different.

It became clear to us very early on that Canavan took no s**t and, in the beginning, he wasn't that high up on our list of best buddies.

We made some silly mistake though. Or at least I did.

On one occasion, he caught me spitting on the floor inside the school. In hindsight a really stupid thing to do. I was a cocky teenage lad with no common sense. There are quite a number of ways to describe exactly what happened next. But, for want of a better way to phrase it... Canavan let me know exactly what he thought of that act. He went through me for a shortcut. Here I was getting verbally torn apart by the next icon of gaelic football. I really didn't feel too clever after that. What the hell was I thinking about?

It was probably the first time in my life that someone properly challenged my bad behaviour in a school setting. It marked a boundary for me. A lesson learned. I couldn't get away with doing anything like that again.

Canavan was setting out the ground rules and I knew exactly where I stood. It took him quite some time to warm to me after that. He'd probably claim that he never has. Happier times with Canavan would come later.

AS I NEARED my sixteenth birthday, I became more and more interested in hearing how my uncles were getting on out in the United States. I was convinced that there were opportunities for me out there and school was just one big obstacle to me getting out there some day.

A lifeline was just around the corner.

Donal Campbell came in one day and spoke to us. He had news for us.

'Look boys, listen up.

'The exams start in the second week of May, and we normally let the Year 12s go home from that date onwards to study and sit the tests.

'School isn't over until the middle of May, but you boys can get away two weeks ahead of that.'

It was as if someone had just taken the leash off us. We were out the door and free. Silly teenagers thinking that the world was now our oyster. I actually spent some time at home during the next couple of weeks doing small amounts of study and I ended up sitting all the statutory GCSE exams.

It will come as no surprise that they didn't go well for me.

I did manage to pass Technology, Music and Physical Education. Failed basically everything else. It's funny how those three subjects, Technology, Music and PE would not only influence but dominate the rest of my life.

Word of advice kids.

Study hard in school kids, and you'll end up passing the exams that will carry you forward for the rest of your life. I'm living proof of that.

Three exam passes.

It was a bleak outcome.

I needed a new focus.

My father was out making money and that's what I wanted to do. In our family we had all the love that we needed as kids. Exams were never seen as the be-all and end-all.

If you didn't take the initiative yourself, then that's too bad. Move on… look for another opportunity. Don't sit around waiting for something to happen… get up off your arse and make it happen.

Get your priorities right.

So that's exactly what I did.

My next priority was getting a job and making money.

AS TEENAGERS, WE never let a weekend pass without at least one night-time excursion into 'the town' as we called it. Cookstown on a Friday, Saturday and

Sunday night offered the kind of sights and sounds that weren't just as plentiful in rural Ardboe.

Hard to beat a healthy social life.

Despite our young years, the alcohol flowed and the conversation was enhanced to new levels of intellect as a result of the consumption of some questionable beverages. In the United States, fake IDs are a must but they were only an optional extra in County Tyrone. Whilst we made the most of any chance to go out, Saturday nights were the most hazardous for us.

Saturday nights had a huge knock-on effect on Sunday mornings.

Sunday morning meant one thing in our house.

Mass!

My mother was a traditionalist. There was no compromise whatsoever. It didn't matter where you were the previous night. It didn't matter what else you had on. If you valued your health, then you were going to mass.

There were two masses in our parish on a Sunday morning. The early mass in Moortown… or the later mass in Ardboe.

Almost inevitably, the later we arrived back in from Cookstown, the higher the likelihood was that you were going to be launched out of your bed on the Sunday morning for the early mass in Moortown. My mother never drank or smoked. That resulted in very little appreciation, or sympathy, for the kind of hangover that we might be suffering from.

Bed offered us an oasis of hope for a full recovery.

No, sympathy wasn't plentiful. Neither was the moaning and whinging of mostly the boys in our house when she marched through the bedroom door and threw open the bedroom curtains. After several shouts and calls for us to get up, all negotiating terms and conditions had ceased by the point.

She's an absolute angel in my eyes. How she put up with us, I've absolutely no clue.

Mass was often a struggle, but we attended. As an Irish family living in Ardboe it was a central part of our lives; if I was at home visiting now, there would still be a firm expectation that I should still be in attendance there… every Sunday.

WHILE FOOTBALL PLAYED a big part of my teenage life, music was fast becoming a close second. At school, Master Pat Casey took me under his wing. Pat was an incredible fiddle (violin) player, but he could play almost any instrument, from a harmonica through to a guitar. He had a deep appreciation for traditional Irish music and was an extremely talented musician.

As a fledging guitar player, I was quickly drawn to him.

Pat and I hit it off immediately. I felt that he could identify with me. As a teenager from the lough shore in Ardboe I was rough around the edges but I just felt that Pat got the way of me and understood how he could get the best out of me.

Pat was the man who helped me to set up and record my first album. It was produced in memory of one of my own school mates, Mark Heagney.

Mark was a phenomenal boxing talent and lived in Kildress, just a few miles to the west of Cookstown. On January 9, 1994, Mark lost his life in a serious car accident not far from his home. He died alongside another two young men, the Lagan brothers, Martin and Paddy.

Those deaths rocked our school community to its very foundations. There was a profound sense of shock and loss. That type of devastation would mark other aspects of my life.

Martin, Paddy and Mark were very popular guys and all three were very well known to the school staff and the vast majority of students who attended the school.

The utter devastation of losing a school mate so young left us all feeling helpless. And yet, it's at exactly a time like this that I find I'm sparked into action from a song writing perspective. I'm a bit of a sponge during those times.

The words and phrases of others circle around, and I capture and synthesise them into verses.

Sometimes, it's the words and phrases that lead to notes and chords. Sometimes it's the other way around. Moments like the loss of Mark Heagney, someone that I knew so well, slots me into song writing mode.

Mark Heagney was a talented boy,
Boxing was his pride and joy.
Tears of sorrow, cry of pain
For what we have lost
What God has gained.

IT WAS CLEAR that I was never going to leave Holy Trinity College with a folder full of exam passes to my name. My teachers knew that just as well as I did. Some more than others spotted some kind of talent in me and none more so than my music teacher.

Collette Dinsmore was my music teacher and, much like Pat Casey, we got on really well. Collette helped to strengthen my love of music and she helped me become a technically better guitar player.

I spent a lot of time in Collette's classroom. She used to make up all number of extravagant excuses as to why I was there when I quite clearly should not have been. She had a huge influence on my music.

Every couple of years the school would organise and run a fundraising event. Sometimes it was a school production of one of the well-known musicals. Sometimes it was just a talent show with several different students performing their pieces.

One thing was consistent throughout; it was always very well supported by the local community. The college hall was always packed out for shows.

A few of us decided to form a band to take part in the show. Mark Heagney's passing brought us together and the school show gave us the opportunity that we needed to perform.

Step forward… The College Kids.

The band was made up of Peter James Kelly, who was a cousin of mine from Ardboe. Ciaran McCrory from Kildress, Anthony Glackin, and James McGarrity from Cookstown and myself.

The extent of our fame was really only meant to last no longer than the one or two nights playing for parents and the wider Cookstown community, but a couple of us soon spotted a wider market for our musical expertise.

We had some big ideas. Stadium gigs and Glastonbury would certainly form part of future possibilities, but first we were all about securing some fast money and that meant getting into the pubs and clubs in Cookstown.

Our first proper gig was in the Black Horse bar in Cookstown. Capacity of about 100 people. We probably maxed the place out the first night, and that without the advent of social media. The Black Horse soon became our regular Friday night gig.

Anthony Glackin's father, Gerry, played in a band called the Irish Brigade. He was our key man to get up and running; Gerry had all the gear that we couldn't afford.

The College Kids had an extensive repertoire.

Five songs! That called for a little improvisation. By the end of the night, the songs would have been repeated at least five times. We had a well thought out plan though. We would repeat the songs in a different order, and hope that the locals would be too intoxicated to notice.

Perhaps we are the reason the *Hills of Donegal* became such a popular number in the heart of County Tyrone.

Apart from the Black Horse gigs and one or two other 'guest appearances' at a few other establishments in and around East Tyrone, the lifespan of The College Kids was limited, but music for me was everywhere I went. My grandmother's home was the epicentre for music sessions in Ardboe. Every other Monday night people gathered from all parts to granny's house to play music.

Big Tommy O'Neill also had a positive influence on me as a musician. Tommy was a local legend and a wonderful guitar player. He was a regular visitor to my grandmother's house when I was a kid. I never failed to pick up a chord or learn a thing, or song or two, when Tommy was around.

By the end of my teenage years, I could handle the guitar and play almost anything you want. Those music sessions gave me the skill and confidence to hold my own with some of the best of local traditional Irish music talent.

My experimentation with song writing continued, but the lure of football was still strong. I found that after a while I wasn't devoting enough time to practice. With me it's always all of nothing.

I'd have been the kind of person that would give one thing one hundred percent, and most times to the detriment of something else that I was trying to do. Music was a hobby.

Kicking football in the Little Bronx or on the GAA pitches of Tyrone and beyond meant that balancing the two was a challenge sometimes beyond me. I'd only discover later in life that I had the ability to balance the two.

It was only then that I gained an insight into how both could be mutually beneficial to both my social and business circles.

PART 3

911

THAT EVENING, ERIN climbed the stairs, as she liked to watch some of her favourite shows on her iPad in bed before I came up to the room.

Early mornings mean early nights in our home.

I normally watched the Irish news on the TV downstairs. That was just a normal thing. An opportunity for me to touch base with the news and goings on in Ireland. It always kept me grounded and well informed.

I was able to join in most conversations with friends and family at home because I was across the detail. Irish sport or politics, it mattered not.

My finger was always on the pulse. Little did I know how precious that pulse was to me, as I parked my backside into my favourite seat that night.

This is Erin's recollection of my missing hours…

'I COULD JUST about make out some sort of muffled sound, before Mickey was at the door.

He just stood there and said… 'ERIN'.

'I knew something was wrong immediately. "Jesus Christ… what's wrong with you Mickey? You definitely went too hard on the run tonight. Just lay down for a minute."

'A few seconds later, he said that it was going away. And then it came back with a bang. All I could think of was Oh My God… *this is serious*. He was in trouble and he needed my help.

'I reached for my phone… and dialled 911… "I think my husband is having a heart attack. We need your help. His chest is really sore. He says that his jaw is really hurting. He's only 41 years old… he just got back from a run".

'Everything that I said to the operator led her to the same conclusion. Mickey was in serious trouble. "We are sending emergency service first responders over to you right away... they are on their way," she assured.

'When the call ended, I turned to Mickey and said, "You want to put on a shirt?" The stupid things that go through your head.

'I wanted to get him downstairs, as the children were sleeping and I didn't want them to wake up. I knew that he wasn't well, but I couldn't get my head around the fact that my 41-year-old husband was having a heart attack.

'Surely it must be something else?

'He's only... 41!'

'WHEN WE GOT downstairs, Mickey dropped to his knees and crouched down beside an ottoman beside the couch in the sitting room.

'Two cops came in through the door just a few seconds later. They kind of just stood there and looked at him for a minute.

'They had a bag with them.

'Mickey reached out his hand... "Lads... can somebody help me here".

'As soon as he said that, he just dropped out cold on the floor.

'I just remember screaming.

'One of the cops raced over to Mickey, but as he tried to stop... the mat under him slipped on the wooden floor... he crashed to the floor.

'Thankfully, he wasn't hurt.

'He got to work on Mickey as quickly as he could. As he did, an ambulance pulled into the driveway. The policeman shouted at his colleague to tell the paramedics to get in here as quick as they could.

'The lead paramedic raced into the house and went straight to work on Mickey with the chest compressions and the shocks.

'Then, suddenly, incredibly... Mickey opened his eyes.

'He was awake, but he was very aggressive and combative. It was like he was possessed by some kind of demon.

'What the hell is going on here?' I asked one of the EMT's.

'No one spoke to me.

'I got ushered into the kitchen by the second cop... and he started asking me for my ID. I didn't know if he was trying to distract me or was genuinely trying to work out if I was who I said I was.

'Why the hell are you trying to reach into my bag?'

'MY HEAD WAS in a mess.

'I was freaking out.

'No one was telling me anything… and this cop wanted me to prove that I was ME.

'They spent about 10 minutes working on him.

'He was still very aggressive as they tried to move him onto the stretcher. As they moved him out of the house towards the ambulance, one of the cops asked me for the keys to my car. They wanted to move it in order to get the ambulance closer to the house.

'I tried to get alongside the stretcher as they moved him through the doorway and out onto the porch… but they told me to stop.

'COVID restrictions meant I wasn't allowed to accompany him to the hospital… I'd have to drive myself.

The kids! What am I going to do with the kids?

'My question was answered as Maureen Conroy opened the front door.

'Gerald and Maureen Conroy, both of whom are Irish and who also set up home in Pearl River, had spotted all the lights and commotion going on across the street. Maureen said that she would look after the kids and clean the place up.

'It was a mess… medical packaging and throw-away equipment laying around all over the place.'

'I GOT INTO Mickey's car and pointed it in the direction of the hospital.

'All I could think of was that Mickey is going to be so embarrassed about all of this. He was awake when he left the house. I'd just left the scene of a major trauma.

Thank God, they have him back.

'They will give him whatever he needs… I'll have him back home with me again later tonight… or tomorrow.'

LATER, IT WAS confirmed later that I flatlined once in the house and twice in the ambulance on the way to the hospital.

LUCKILY FOR ME, there were two emergency room specialist cardiac doctors on duty that night at Montefoire Nyack Hospital.

I'd arrived in the ambulance just as Dr Greenhut was ending his shift, and Dr Alejandro was taking over.

Erin was ushered into a side room when she arrived at the hospital by Dr Greenhut.

The news wasn't good…

'Your husband is very, very seriously ill.

'He's had a very serious heart attack.

'His heart stopped three times.

'Once at your house.

'Twice in the ambulance on the way here.

'Do you understand how serious this is?'

'The third time that your husband's heart stopped… they weren't able to bring him back until they got here… to the hospital.'

I'VE JUST STARED long and hard at those words.

It's feels like I'm writing about some other person.

I was gone. My God… I was gone in the ambulance.

For how many minutes, I don't know. The facts are that at some point in that ambulance I flatlined for a third time, and a number of minutes passed before they brought me back to life inside the Emergency Room in the hospital.

How can it be?

How can it really be that a lifeless body is stretchered into an Emergency

Room and they can intubate it... and power it back to life?

How the heck can that person be me?

The paramedics in the ambulance tried to intubate me, but Dr Alejandro managed to do it when he got me into the ER. He saved my life. He gave me back hopes... dreams and my future with my beautiful wife and children.

He never met me.

It didn't matter.

In a few short moments with the great skills in the world... he gave me my future.

But I had work to do.

Meanwhile, Erin was still trying... desperately trying to understand.

'I had no idea what I was being told.

'Dr Alejandro said my acceptance of the situation was admirable, but in truth... I was in shock... numbed by the news that I had just received.

'That shock intensified when I was brought into the ER after they had finished working on Mickey.

'His whole face was black and blue.

'This is not the man that left our house.

'That's when it hit me the hardest.

How can he recover from this?

'I got really scared.

This is not good.

'I stood there, staring at him... repeating the same line over and over again in my head.'

This is not good.

A SHORT TIME later, Erin contacted her mother and her stepdad, and repeated that line again.

By that point I had been placed in sedation and a surgeon by the name of Dr Greenberg was getting everything ready to take me to theatre to insert a stent.

Before that procedure, he met with Erin and he told her that he was on call that night staying in a hotel close by. By that stage, Erin really wasn't processing everything that she was being told. Understandable, given the circumstances.

Dr Greenberg was very good to my wife. He asked her what kind of a person

I was? She explained that I took my fitness very seriously and that we had two young children, two and five years old.

The process to insert stents into the heart does carry a risk of complications but these are normally small in most cases.

I wasn't in the 'most cases' category.

Erin was told that things might not go okay.

Dr Greenberg introduced Erin to the team of nurses who were there to support him. There was one last opportunity for Erin to see me before they took me into the theatre.

I was still very heavily sedated... I don't recall any of that.

DR GREENBERG WALKED into the waiting room to talk with Erin just over two hours later.

He explained to her that he was able to get a stent into my artery and that the extent of the plaque rupture was one of the worst that he had ever seen.

It's difficult for me even now to reconcile that, while I'd been attempting to keep fit, that something smaller than the width of an artery was building up inside of me.

Threatening to kill me.

In the run up to that day, I hadn't once felt lethargic or unwell. I may have had a slight bit of indigestion or heartburn but I always but that down to something I'd ate... something spicy or very rich.

It would come and go every now and then, but it wasn't significant or something that bothered me to the point that I'd ever get worried about it; nothing of any severity that would lead me to think that my life would be thrown into turmoil.

Three weeks prior to the widow-maker, I had a physical with my doctor.

My bloods and electrocardiogram (EKG) were all clear. Crucially, however, I hadn't undertaken the dye test for plaque in the arteries.

The procedure to insert the stent in the Cath lab had shown up a piece of plaque that had ruptured and came off the wall of my left anterior descending artery (LAD).

The LAD is the largest coronary artery.

It branches from the left main coronary artery. It's job it to carry oxygenated blood to the left side of your heart.

The plaque had entirely blocked the LAD artery, leading to what's commonly known as the widow-maker heart attack. The survival chances for anyone who suffers a widow-maker outside of a hospital 6%.

... 6%.

A 94% chance of death.

That's how close I came.

Dr Greenberg reassured Erin that they had done absolutely everything they could to treat my heart, but that wasn't all the news that he had for her. Due to the length of time between my third flatline and my resuscitation, they were not sure if there was any brain damage.

THE ROCKLAND GAELIC Athletic Association grounds and facility looked different from this vantage point.

I could make out the car park, the clubhouse… and the playing field.

My eyes were drawn to a large congregation of people gathered in silence. They were in prayer.

Their prayers were for me.

With that realisation, I was overcome with an energy pulling me across the clubhouse roof and out across the playing field. It was the most beautiful feeling that I've ever felt in my life.

Pure serenity.

Peaceful.

Calm.

It's difficult to put into words how good it felt. I was drawn to that energy. I wanted to go towards that energy.

Nothing else mattered. I wanted to go there.

Then, suddenly, another force of a very different kind of energy captured me. This time the force was pulling me back. It was telling me not to go there.

Two forces… pulling me in different directions.

Pure serenity.

Pure and simple serenity.

And in their darkest, most challenging moments of life, where from the outside we can say God doesn't exist… in the trenches of suffering, that is when people will tell you they've found him.

(Fr Brendan Fitzgerald, The Bronx, New York)

I OPENED MY eyes.

Blurred figures that I couldn't focus on.

Light and shadows in a haziness of confusion.

Confusion broken by the sound of a familiar voice… Fr Brendan Fitzgerald. A Kerry man originally from Tralee, now living in the Bronx. He was standing above me. His hand was on my head. He was praying over me.

In the midst of the hazy vision, the words broke through with clarity.

'You are going to be okay Mickey. Everything is in God's hands.'

Those words will never leave me.

Then darkness… and silence.

I'm told that I fell quickly back to sleep again after that. I was still on the ventilator and in a medically induced coma. That event must have triggered the doctor's decision to try and back me out of the sedation the next day.

My earliest memory of that was the sound and extremely uncomfortable sensation of a suction tube moving through my throat. The medical staff were removing the ventilator tubes.

That sound was followed by a more familiar voice of Erin reassuring me that

I was going to be okay.

'MICKEY!!

'MICKEY!!"

'Please try to relax. Everything is going to be okay.

'Mickey, you took a heart attack. You took a widow-maker heart attack.

'But you survived it.

'Everything is going to be okay.'

THE NURSE TOLD Erin that I wouldn't hear her.

I've news for her… I heard her loud and clear.

Everything in terms of what I could see and take in was foggy. However, I do recall the sound of that suction tube being used to clear my throat and mouth.

I'm relying on others to fill in the blanks here, but I'm told that I had developed pneumonia and I was still in a very dangerous state of health.

When I reached a point of semi-consciousness, I just remember thinking… I should not be here.

Where the hell… is here?

The next memory is one in the aftermath of wakening up from that coma. It's perhaps the most painful and humiliating. I had emptied my bowels all over the hospital bed. Erin was left to help clean me up.

Rock bottom.

I've never felt so sorry for myself… utterly helpless.

I couldn't believe that I was in that position.

I couldn't believe that I put Erin into this position.

Am I really this weak?

I couldn't speak… I couldn't move a single muscle. It's the realisation of what's happened that's the most crushing aspect of all of this. The realisation that I was in for the fight of my life. Looking back at it with some clarity now, I realise that I'd slipped into survival mode.

I'd only two options.

Fight and live… or curl up in a ball and die.

PULSE

*I JUST LAY there still in the bed. My mind in turmoil.
I knew that I had to find a way to go to the toilet
myself the next time. I couldn't put Erin into that
position again.*

*Without knowing it, I'd set my very first goal on
the road to recovery. That was it. That simple.*

But I was in a bad place.

*My liver was failing. My kidneys had almost
packed up... and I had pneumonia.*

*I had just woken up from something that I
shouldn't have woken up from and I found myself in a
battle to just breathe, never mind live.*

*Somewhere along the line, Erin came into the
room with an iPad. She told me that there was
something that she wanted me to see.*

'Can you watch this here with me Mickey?

*'They are having a healing mass for you tonight... in
Rockland GAA.' I turned my head towards her and said
in a weakened voice. 'I know... I've already seen it.'*

*At the time Erin gave my words little or no notice.
I was on heavy medication and for the most part not
thinking or talking too straight.*

But I had... I'd seen it.

I'd somehow witnessed it... before it happened.

ALL OF THIS, backed up with the reality that I was still suffering from swelling on the brain. Also known as 'Pump head'. More common to people in the aftermath of serious road accidents where there's a degree of trauma. Those early days after coming out of sedation brought several instances of short-term memory loss.

I've been through this all several times with Erin since then. She tells me that she can't remember hearing my words, but I'm convinced that I said it.

I'm now in a position whereby I'm not sure if I thought it, or said it to her verbally. My mind has somehow convinced me that I did.

Did I see that healing mass before it actually took place?

Pure serenity and that beautiful energy.

Call it what you want. Call it whatever way you are comfortable with. My reality is this…

On Monday, March 29, 2021 my heart flatlined three times.

Once in my house and twice in the ambulance that raced me to Montefiore Nyack Hospital. My reality is that somewhere amidst those three episodes and the two-day coma that I was in, I experienced something few have ever witnessed.

I experienced what being called away from this life looks like in glorious technicolour.

Let me be absolutely clear about this…

I'm not ready to die.

I'm now not afraid to either.

AFTER BEING ADMITTED to hospital, my brother, Raymond was right there with me. He only left the room for minutes at a time to use the bathroom or get something to eat, during his stays that could last all day. And yet in those moments, I would turn to Erin and ask… 'Where's Raymond?

'Why isn't Raymond here?'

'Will Raymond come here at all?'

Heavy medication was doing strange things to my mind. How did I see that Rockland mass before it happened?

By that time, my sister, Andrea and my mother, Teresa had made the journey from Ireland out to see me, after getting special dispensation to travel during the Covid pandemic. The first time that they walked into the room was tough.

I felt so helpless that all I could do was hug my mother for several minutes. Lying in that bed, all I could see on her face was a reflection of the state I was in. And yet at the same time, I was so thankful to have her and Andrea there.

I needed something to root me to this earth. I asked Fr Brendan to say the rosary with me because I'd felt a serious spiritual shift in those days.

I wouldn't have been a regular attender of Mass, though I would have gone sporadically, and like many Irish, I seemed to always be at weddings and funerals.

I always had a lot of personal faith but, like many, I had a problem with the Catholic Church and what it stood for. Child abuse scandals and how they ignored or didn't deal with them is a problem a lot of us have.

Fr Brendan started the Rosary, but I led a good part of it. We used to say the Rosary in my grandmother's house and not since she passed away would I have led prayers.

When we were finished, I told everyone again of what I had seen in Rockland. This was real. I saw it all.

I felt it and I was trying to convey just what had happened.

It was awkward in a sense. In that, people would not associate me with talking about a spirituality. I find it hard to believe myself. But even now I feel moved by what has been massive shift of spiritual awakening within me.

I AM NOT afraid to die now.

I've said that to Erin. But I am also not ready to die.

My life contains a purpose that I have to fulfil and I have two lovely children and a wonderful wife. I'm not ready to die. I've a lot of living to do.

Two days after I came off sedation, I got out of bed to go to the toilet. First goal achieved.

They brought the commode to the side of the bed. That happened only once. The next time I used the walking stick they provided and I made it out to the toilet by myself. Second goal achieved. Small victories.

Monumental victories.

Derek supervised the walk across to the toilet but I made it there and back on my own. The big thing that hit me around that time was exactly how fatigued and unfit I really was. This heart attack had rocked my very foundation.

The Ejection Fraction (EF) is used to measure how well your left or right ventricle pumps blood during each heartbeat. A normal EF is anywhere between 50% and 75%. My EF status at that time was just 30%.

That means I was in the status of heart failure.

Parts of my skin were yellow and grey. Other parts of my legs and arms were black. The pupils of my eyes were red and my eyeballs were swollen and felt like they were bulging out of my eye sockets.

I was sore from the emergency stents procedure. My chest was sore from the compressions. I was hoarse from all the tubes down my throat. That fire in my throat meant that I was sucking lozenges most of the time for well over a week. It felt like the worst strep throat that you could ever have, multiplied by five.

I was a train wreck. And somehow, none of that mattered. I just had it in my head that I was going to beat this physically. A fire ignited inside of me. I can't explain how or why. I f**king knew, I just knew inside my head that I was going to beat this. The two boys were at the front of my mind throughout that thought process.

I need to be around for my children.

That became a permanent mantra… over and over inside my head.

I didn't want people sitting around my bed feeling sorry for me. I wanted to be seeing all of these people in good times.

I needed to get out of that bed and there was still no certainty of that. In the first few days after I came out of the coma, it was about trying to get my arms moving. It would take every ounce of energy just to do that.

In my mind it was just about trying to get some kind of motion back into my body. The doctors and nurses had a number of small tests for me to see where I was mentally. I aced all of the tests… counting from one to 20. Counting backwards from 20 to one.

Naming the President and Vice President of the United States.

Reciting the alphabet.

The capital of New York? I got one answer wrong. They asked me what month it was? I told them that it was March. Wrong. It was April. In the great traditions of the GAA, Derek and Raymond lodged an appeal. I had, after all, taken the heart attack on March 29.

It was an honest mistake. The nurse restored my 100% record.

I was winning all the breaking balls.

HISSSSSSSSSS...
OOOOOOO...

HISSSSSSSSSS...
OOOOOOO...

HISSSSSSSSSS...
OOOOOOO...

HISSSSSSSSSS...
OOOOOOO...

HISSSSSSSSSS....

ALL YOU HEAR.

A mask covering my mouth, pumping oxygen up my nose.

Second after second.

Minute after minute.

Hour after hour.

I just lay there, with no energy to spare... exhausted and spent.

That hissing sound will haunt me to the day I die. Every wakened hour was filled with thoughts of getting better.

Somethings helped, beyond measure.

One day, Erin arrived in with a video on her iPad.

Peter Canavan had arranged something. Typical Canavan, he had gathered up a number of our Tyrone team that won the 2003 All-Ireland Championship to make a few messages to send to me.

First up on the video was the famously bald Canavan. He is wearing a wig; sort of like Brian May of Queen and he is complaining about the barbers being closed during the pandemic. I played it over and over again.

Some of these men I hadn't seen in 10 years, but they were all here on my iPad, rooting for me. That video became instantly precious. I had the drive to get better, but this… this gave me instant energy.

Then, there were the medical staff around me, all great sources of inspiration and strength for throughout. They were all very special people but one of them appeared to be heaven sent.

Erin has a music school she runs down in Woodlawn, in the Bronx, named the Erin Loughran School of Irish Music and Arts.

One of Erin's students was a young girl called Sarah Lynch. Sarah attended Erin's school from she wasn't much more than a toddler. Sarah was just 17 when she very tragically passed away in a car accident in New York on Monday, February 15, 2021.

Her father is Shane Lynch, originally from Direen in Cahersiveen, and her mother is Joanne, who comes from Derriana, Dromid. Great Kerry people.

Sarah and her family were very well known in Irish American circles in New York. Sarah was our child-minder. She came with us on music cruises.

To Erin, she was like a wee sister.

She meant so much to us and we were devastated when she passed away so suddenly. It was a massive shock and very hard on Erin in particular.

When I was still under sedation, Erin spoke with Sarah's mummy, Joanne. It was during that time that Joanne told Erin that she would pray to Sarah for me… to watch over me and look after me.

The following morning Erin awoke in the waiting room close to my bedroom in the Intensive Care Unit in the hospital. When she made her way into my room, she discovered that there was a new nurse looking after me.

Erin was drawn to her immediately. She has shared with me since that the new nurse was absolutely amazing. She was extremely attentive towards me and she did a wonderful job looking after me during that time.

Almost overcome by the attentiveness and great care that this nurse showed to me, Erin approached her.

'Hello, I'm Erin… I'm Mickey's wife. What is your name?'

The nurse replied, 'Lovely to meet you, Erin… my name is Sarah'.

We since learned that Nurse Sarah had five children of her own. Sarah, and an Indian nurse called Bibi, were absolutely amazing during my time in ICU.

As I got better, and energy levels increased Erin gave me back my phone.

It was an avalanche.

Jesus Christ of Almighty.

Almost too much to comprehend.

My WhatsApp and text message icons had hundreds and hundreds of numbers beside them… messages from Oisin McConville, Tommy Griffin, Tomas Ó Sé…

How did those men even know who I am? I was no star on the football field. Hundreds and hundreds and hundreds of messages… Video messages… WhatsApp messages.

This was bad. I actually died… *I actually died.*

Next, I started reading social media which led me on to newspaper articles. Everywhere… an outpouring of support from all over Ireland. All over the Irish American community… people from all corners of everywhere sending messages.

My heart attack had an impact on people in all corners of the world.

In the middle of it all was Erin. She told me how she had spent time responding to messages on the phone before having to give up for a while due to the numbers. If it wasn't phone messages, it was lifting mail from the house. A house filling up with food and flowers arriving from *everywhere.* Then, there were the newspapers who were contacting her for updates.

I know now, that was a stressful time for her because she wasn't in a position to meet their demands for updates.

One of the standout messages that I got was sent to me was from a close friend of ours, Oliver O'Connell of Clare. He is an accordion player, and he spent a lot of his time writing poetry and songs. Oliver has his own troubles and he is gone through some tough times. He lost his wife to cancer a few years back.

When he penned the letter to me, Oliver was in hospital himself. I wasn't aware of that until well after I got home. It was a two-page letter. He began by telling me that he was thinking about me and Erin and the two kids. He told me of his own experience in dealing with and getting his head around the fact that he had cancer.

In the letter, Oliver described how, the night before a scan, he took a blank book and he wrote for 10 hours. In the book, he wrote about not having any cancer in his body. The following day the medical staff scanned him and they found no sign of cancer in his body.

This was a man in a very similar position to me, having suffered a lot of trauma, giving me advice on how to recover. He advised me to not talk about the heart attack, because... every time I did, I was wasting my time.

In his words, 'The tsunami has arrived. You can't relive that but you can pick up the pieces and get on with life. Every time you wasted recalling what happened, you'll end up back inside that tsunami again.'

Oliver insisted this causes depression and slows down the healing process. It was so true. It was the best advice that I've ever got since the beginning of all of this. I made a conscious decision after reading Oliver's letter that I would not dwell on my sickness. I would only look forward to my healing process, along with my diet and the mental battles that lay ahead.

FOR TWO WEEKS prior to reading that letter, I cried every single day.

I cried in front of Erin.

When people called with me in the hospital I'd put on a face and be strong with them. Whenever they would leave, I'd break down crying again. All of those tears came from the realisation of what really happened to me. The realisation that I should be dead. The realisation of... what if I left my wife and two boys behind?

Simply, it was the early stages of depression.

Those messages, letters and videos drove me on. It wasn't long until I got my mind focused on the type of food that I was eating. I started on a low sodium Mediterranean diet made up mainly of fish and vegetables. I wanted to go a step further than that.

I got onto my phone and started to research plant-based foods.

I wanted to know the best way to heal heart disease. I didn't want to be living with chronic illness all of my life. I knew that this was serious, and I wanted to fix it.

We were on a roll. At one point Derek came in later with a razor and suggested that he shave me? That didn't go down to well with the nurse looking after me.

She told him that my blood was like water and that if he nicked my chin with the blade, I'd bleed to death. She snapped the razor out of Derek's hand and went away talking to herself.

The job was abandoned but, a few short hours, Derek appeared back with an electric razor.

He wasn't going to be beaten.

As I got a little bit more mobile, I started to turn my attention to researching how I could make myself better. Erin was already beginning to stop of at some of the plant-based food shops in Nyack.

She was bringing me in various different combinations of that type of food. It gave me something to focus on because I wasn't really in a position to do much else. I needed to concentrate on my nutrition and build up my strength.

That was all backed up by prayer. My sister-in-law, Neidin, Ned as we know her, brought me in Rosary beads. I prayed the Rosary every night. I stared death in the face and now I reckoned this was the time to start praying again. There was nearly always someone in the hospital room with me, but I still felt that I was alone.

Me against this heart attack… and me against the place that it had left me in.

All of that gave me energy and all of that was backed up with the support that I had from Erin. The strength that she showed throughout that ordeal was phenomenal.

THROUGHOUT THOSE DAYS in hospital, the doctors confirmed that I had suffered an enormous heart attack event and that it was going to take a long time to recover. They told me that there was a lot of damage done to my heart and that I might not ever fully recover from that.

That brought me back to a time when I broke my leg playing for Ardboe senior footballers against Aghyaran in October 2006. It happened on a cold wet night down in Ardboe. Benny Hurl and Roger Keenan were the managers of that team and I remember Benny shaking his head when he saw the injury.

I was taken by ambulance down to Craigavon Area Hospital… 40 minutes away. The doctors at Craigavon told me that they could do nothing for me there…

I was moved to the RVH in Belfast.

I woke up after the surgery and was told by the surgeon, 'Mickey, your footballing career is over'. I was 27 years old at the time and it was a statement that I just could not accept.

Within six months I was back running again and, in 2007, I won the 'Footballer of the Year' award within my own club. All I needed to hear was that I wasn't going to play football again.

Suddenly, that cardiac ICU room in Montefoire Nyack Hospital New York was linked to an RVH ward in Belfast.

Those words associated with not being able to fully recover kick-started my pathway to healing myself again. That process would require my faith to be stronger than it ever was before. I needed those prayers, and I needed to accept that I'd been offered an opportunity to still be alive.

Those were the key components required to make this happen.

After 12 days I was moved out of the High Dependency ICU, into an ICU hospital room.

I didn't speak to a single other patient during that time.

Where I was at in ICU at that time, I was probably the only patient that walked out of it. There was no one up there that was in any fit shape to talk.

I spent two days in that new ICU room, and it was there I met my eldest son, Micháel for the first time since... everything. Erin managed to slip him past security and up to my room... I hadn't seen him in two weeks.

He jumped straight up into the bed beside me.

That was the moment I fully realised that I needed to get out of there. I hugged the life out of him and planted a hundred kisses on him.

Unbeknownst to Erin, a security guard had spotted Erin taking him in. He followed her up to the room. When he got to the room, he saw me hugging my son and crying with happiness to hold him.

I will be forever grateful to him for what he did next.

When he saw what was happening, he thought, *It's a father with his son. I shouldn't be here.* He walked out the door.

When the time came to go home, a nurse arrived at the beside and spoke to Erin and I.

'Mickey I cannot believe that you are getting home. I was on duty here the night that you came in… I worked on you for six and a half minutes.' She told us that the call came in that evening that a 41-year-old male was on route to the hospital.

When I was taken into the Emergency Room, they saw that I had a wedding ring on my finger and they assumed that I was married with kids. She told me that the team said that they needed to work hard to keep this man alive. That's exactly what they did.

DRESSED IN A Rockland GAA jersey and tracksuit bottoms, I was wheeled out of the hospital. When the doors slid open, the air felt like it was filled with gold dust.

I got out of the wheelchair and propped myself up close to the car with my walking stick. Erin insisted that she took a photo at that point.

That photo would make one or two social media posts and news outlets a few hours later.

When the passenger door of the car closed, I turned to Erin…

'Get me home to my kids.'

PART **4**

Goals

WHEN I LEFT school, only two things had my full attention.

Football and Music.

In that order.

My sporting passion was doing absolutely everything in my power to get onto the starting team of Ardboe senior gaelic football team.

As an amateur side, that bit wasn't about making money. It was about representing your family and friends on the local team.

Gaelic football in our part of the world was a type of tribal warfare. It was all about putting one over on your neighbours, and teams across the county. Above all, it was about winning.

Ardboe O'Donovan Rossa gaelic football team had always been a very successful side on the Tyrone club scene. By the time I was ready to stake my claim for a place on the senior team, Ardboe had already six Tyrone Senior Football Championship titles.

THE TYRONE SENIOR Football Championship is everything for a club player in Tyrone.

Ardboe won their first senior championship in 1968 when they were captained by 'The King' Frank McGuigan. The club would go on to secure another three titles in the 70s, winning three in-a-row... 1971, '72 and '73. In the 80s they added another two titles in 1984 and '87.

That led to one of the first problems that I had.

I was trying to get gain a place on a team in the mid 90s that was already full of proven winners.

Yes, some of them were closer to the end of their careers than the start of it. But getting noticed and considered by the management team wasn't going to be an easy task. That required mixing it with some very experienced and battle-hardened individuals, and that was a hazardous task.

My first opportunity to catch the managers eyes was in training. Training meant a lot of running and a lot of skill work with the football in drills. One of the toughest drills at Ardboe senior training was defenders against forwards. All the guys that fancied themselves as defenders lined up on the end line beside the goalposts. The forwards and midfielders would gather around the middle of the field.

I classed myself as a midfielder.

The drill was simple. The ball was kicked out by the goalkeeper and all the forwards and midfielders would compete for it. That was task one.

Win the ball from the kickout between a body of thoroughbreds. If you managed to win the ball, then came task number two.

Winning possession was one thing… holding on to it was another. You would not believe how many things can happen between rising up into the air to catch a ball, and successfully landing with your two feet on the ground.

What would normally take less than a second felt like it went on for a lot longer. Men arrived from everywhere. Arms, legs, shoulders… knees, and elbows. Just about whatever they could use and do, to stop you.

I was only 17 at the time. That meant nothing.

I was able to hold my own.

The moment you won the ball in the air and landed on the ground, there was a big red X on your front, back, side or whatever part of you the Ardboe defenders choose to target. All parts of the ball winner provided a legitimate impact point for an Ardboe defender.

And when they aimed, they didn't miss.

I was the new kid on the block; cocky and carefree. I soon got that knocked out of me. I was there to work, and they were all there to ensure that I worked hard.

It was open warfare. Survival of the fittest.

The Ardboe manager at the time was a schoolteacher, Brendan Convery, who worked in St Pius X High School in Magherafelt as a Physical Education teacher. He was a great character.

He might well have been from the neighbouring county of Derry, but he fitted in very well in Ardboe. He had an Ardboe mentality. At that time training started at 8pm on a Tuesday and Thursday night.

I remember one night being in the changing rooms in Ardboe and looking out at a rotten evening. The rain was hammering down from the heavens and the sky was full of rain clouds that didn't look like they were ever going to disappear. It was cold and miserable.

I can remember thinking, *Please do not bring us to Mickey Mallon's field tonight.*

Mickey Mallon's field ran alongside Ardboe training pitch and there was an incline on it that felt like it was more of a mountain than a hill. Brendan was a plain talker. He arrived in and barked, "Right lads out to f**k... let's go'.

Stevie Coney was one of the more experienced players on the team who had a couple of county senior championship medals at this point. Stevie was sitting beside Paddy McElroy when Brendan made the call to get out the door.

Stevie wasn't impressed.

'Brendan you must be f**king joking. You wouldn't put a milk bottle out that night.' The whole changing room erupted in laughter. About an hour and a half later, the laughing was firmly wiped off all our faces. Mickey Mallon's field had seen to that.

I recall a training session one Sunday morning when I was sent into full-forward to be marked by Benny Hurl. Benny was one of the toughest and hardest players in the county, never mind our club. We are lifelong friends.

Not that day, though. I was always sharp, and I was able to cover the ground quickly. I got out in front of Benny and won the ball. He let me get my hands on the ball but, as soon as I did, a got an unmerciful slap on the side of the ear came my way.

The football spilled free from my hands, and I hit the ground. I immediately pleaded with Brendan Convery, who was refereeing the match, for a free.

Brendan didn't even take me under his notice.

I was just about to get fully upright when, BANG... again. Stevie Coney had just rammed his shoulder into me, and I was down again. The really crazy thing about Stevie Coney hitting me, was that he was actually part of *my* team in the training match.

Cue another plea from me towards Brendan Convery.

Seconds later, I was competing for possession around the midfield area when the veteran Malachy Coyle crashed straight through me. An obvious foul and a free. Once again, Brendan Convery just ignored it.

I learned quickly that there was no point whinging and complaining. I had to toughen up… and I had to toughen up *quickly*. These guys weren't going to step aside and let me take one of their starting jerseys. It was an incredibly intense and brilliant place to learn about what it took to play at that level.

The football was great, and I was as committed to it as anyone else. Gaelic football didn't and doesn't pay the bills though.

I still needed a job.

PULSE

THAT SINKING FEELING.

An empty space inside my chest.

My own personal definition of loneliness.

Sitting there in my armchair in a room full of people, and feeling that I was on my own.

I knew I was very much the centre of their attention, yet I never felt more disconnected from any of them. None of them knew what I was going through.

How could they?

How the hell am I ever going to come back from all of this?

When am I going to feel human again?

I'm alone.

There's no other way to look at this.

Alone.

FRIDAY APRIL 9, 2021 was another picture-perfect day in Rockland County, New York. The sky was the most beautiful colour of bright blue. I was on my way home for the first time since that fateful evening in March.

The previous 12 days had all been a blur.

I couldn't comprehend what had happened to me… difficult to make sense of it all. Was it real? I was shattered, broken and I felt so weak.

Erin was at the wheel of the car, and we shared a few words on how important it was that I get as much rest as possible in the coming days, weeks… and months.

Every yard covered on that journey home felt like a mile.

I couldn't wait to get home to see my children.

When we rounded the corner and into the driveway of our home, I could see that my mother and sister, and my mother-in-law and father-in-law, were all gathered in the house. I opened the passenger door of the car and was greeted by my youngest son, Riordan. He was only two and a half years old at the time. He jumped up onto my lap and rested his head on my chest.

I was overcome with emotion.

I couldn't speak. Riordan didn't speak either.

How could he know what I'd been through? Somehow, in that moment there in the car, he fully understood.

He lay there with his head pressed into my chest for the most of five minutes, motionless and silent. Riordan and I were both more connected now and closer than we had ever been before. In that moment, I knew that both my sons needed me.

For now, I felt washed out… and emptied out. The few steps from the car into the house were tough.

Real tough. Mentally and physically.

I was just rubble in the ruins of my own body.

Between a walking stick, a railing and Erin's help, I negotiated the steps onto the front porch. Three days from my 42nd birthday and here was I, a complete mess.

I shuffled through the front door and past the spot where I had collapsed… just standing there staring at the spot with all the mixed emotions. I returned to the sofa; exact place where the warning pains shot through me.

Around my chest was a heart monitor life vest.

It was fully charged and capable of shocking me… if things took a turn for the worse. I spent most of the rest of the day on the sofa.

When I needed to go to bed, I wouldn't be climbing the stairs – Erin had fixed me up a room downstairs.

I went to bed early that evening, but couldn't sleep.

I lay there listening to the voices of those very familiar to me out in the kitchen. After a while, I could hear them making their way to bed, and Erin came in and joined me in the room. She lay down in the bed beside me and just hugged me. It was like she never wanted to let go of me. She cried so hard.

That was her release valve.

From the moment that I hit the floor at the bottom of the stairs, to this moment, her life had changed as much as mine.

It's been described to me as similar to taking a breath and it rattling around and burning up inside of you for hours, days and weeks.

Suddenly, in that moment Erin was able to release it. So much focus had been on me for the last few weeks, but Erin carried all the burden during that time.

She was living through it every step of the way.

THE FOLLOWING DAY, my two uncles, Brian and Thomas Curran, made their way up from Philadelphia to visit me. Fay Devlin and his wife, Rosemary had also telephoned to check if it was alright to visit.

I was more than happy to see all of them. Their visits gave me a little bolt of energy. A visual assurance that people were rallying around me and supporting me.

My uncle Thomas had experienced a similar event to me while home in Ireland a few years previous. He provided me with reassurance that I could turn this around and get fully back on my feet. Having my two uncles there, along with Fay and Rosemary, really helped take my mind off things for a short time. Fay had been so good to me since I'd made my home in America. His support has been phenomenal.

I suppose he's part of a group of Irishmen that have set up home, and work in this part of the United States. They aren't famous for open shows of affection, touching or verbal. They tend to be more… direct.

'Alright a**hole!

'You've got two weeks, and then you need to get back on the road again.'

I laughed at him. I knew that it was his way of connecting. In truth, the heart attack that I got terrified him. He hoped I'd beat this thing and get back to being me. Privately, I knew different; I could never be the same 'me' again.

There's a real dark side to being sick.

It's such a great leveller in terms of resetting what's important in your life. People visiting me at that time was so important to my sense of worth and well-being. When everyone left that day, it was particularly hard for me.

I CRIED AND wept for about two hours solid, until I couldn't cry anymore. I just couldn't physically cry anymore. I was broken physically, broken mentally.

It almost felt impossible to get out of where I found myself. I never had depression before but this was depression. That severe depression would last for months.

As the hours and days passed, there were numerous occasions that I couldn't stand up. My blood pressure was low, and I just couldn't find any energy whatsoever to do some of the simplest of things… such as lifting a glass, getting out of bed or walking to the door. Getting to the bathroom became a huge ordeal.

I was never on any kind of pill in my life for any kind of illness. But now, if I jumped up and down, you'd have heard my stomach rattle with pills.

My body itself felt like a lump of lifeless meat. *How long am I going to be like this?*

Am I destined to become nothing more than a burden to my family?

The hardest thing was not being able to support Erin with the two boys. I desperately wanted to take both of them out to the backyard and play football with them. I would hear them cry like any other young kids of that age, but all I could do was lie back on the bed and listen.

Frustration mixed with anxiety beyond what I could properly articulate.

So many questions that I'd no answer to.

What does the next week hold for me?

What does the next month hold for me? The next year?

Can I even dare to plan that far ahead?

What I am going to do with my business?

With the people who work for me?

A never-ending spiral of negativity, and hooked up to a walking defibrillator in the form of a life vest.

I was at my lowest point.

THE FIRST STEP on the road back came with confirmation that I was booked onto the Cardiac Rehabilitation Programme which was due to start a fortnight after I came home from hospital.

In the period, just before that, I got a phone call from Paul O'Brien. Paul was a county Tipperary man who had made his home in New York. We had previously done a bit of business together. Paul, like Fay Devlin, is an extremely generous man and someone who has done some tremendous work for the charity, Solace House for a number of years.

Right from the moment he called me on the phone, I knew that he completely got where I was. It was as if he slotted into my mindset. It was the phone call that I needed.

'Mickey, I've been talking to a few of the guys.

'It's very common for people who have survived something similar to you, to have Post Traumatic Stress Disorder.'

His message was simple. It was calm and quietly delivered; he knew exactly where I was at. He told me that there would be much better days ahead.

He reassured me that I had support all around me and that if I had any concerns about the house or my work, that all that I needed to do was to reach out and everything would be taken care of. I needed that.

More accurately, I needed to hear that.

The first thing you have to do, is decide that being optimistic is important to you, because you understand that optimism is essential to fulfilling your dreams and attaining your goals. Once you make that decision, you have to start looking at things from a different perspective.

(Bob Rotella, Sports Psychologist)

A MATTER OF days after walking out of Montefiore Nyack Hospital, I had just walked back through the front door of it again. Here I was, sitting in front in a small office answering consultation questions ahead of my first rehab session.

Shaking.

Nervous.

A thin layer of sweaty moisture forming on my forehead. I'd taken every single step from the car to the front door with the aid of a walking stick. Forty-two years old, and I was relying on a walking stick to support me. I simply hadn't the strength to do anything different.

First up, after the consultation… I got my blood pressure taken.

I dread to think what that figure was… I didn't even ask.

Next… I was ushered out into a rehab gym, hooked up to a heart monitor… and told to get up onto a treadmill. *Are these people crazy? What the hell do they think that I'm going to be able to do on a treadmill?*

Walking.

I was walking like a 90-year-old man on that machine. A few steps. I don't know how many… and then they brought the treadmill belt to a stop.

Next the fear. Fear like I've never ever experienced before.

'Mickey, we are going to increase the pace of this… we need you to raise your heart rate.'

I STOOD THERE. Paralysed with fear.

Raise my heart rate?

It's so hard to explain even now. Until you experience fear like that you will never know.

How am I going to do this?

More questions flood into my distressed mind. *What if that excruciating pain hits me again. Who the heck thinks that this is even a sensible option for me?*

How the hell am I going to survive this?

Even before the belt began to spin under my feet, my heartbeat is raised. Within a few seconds of starting… my heart is thumping.

I can almost see it jumping out of my chest.

My head is telling me to stop. Next, the sweat appears on my forehead. The fear is dripping out of me with every drop of sweat that the rolls down my face.

Anxiety, mixed with depression and fear.

A potent mix.

Next, onto another device, where I had to push a weight out with my hands. The weight was a similar weight to that of a plastic litre bottle of water.

That nearly finished me.

It felt like I was pushing against a brick wall.

Impossible.

Only a few years ago, I was lining out in a county final for Ardboe as strong as an ox. Running around at top speed, crashing into players… jumping out of my skin.

That first day in rehab, I was like a small child trying to get to their feet for the first time. From fear to another dark place. When I got back into the car after that session, I put my head down and held it in my hands.

I flooded up and wept with tears, uncontrollable tears. I shed more during those first few days and weeks than I'd ever cried before in my life.

Uncontrollable tears.

I'd cry until I couldn't cry.

Empty.

Useless.

Emotionally drained.

Cleansed.

Restarting from a place of nothing left to give.

Resetting.

Never doubt the power of being emotionally cleansed. There was a realisation that I was on my own, and that was so hard for me to process. No one could really help me. I was the only person that could fix me. There was no point looking to external sources.

Only I could deal with this.

Me and me alone.

I KNEW THAT I had to go to a new place, deep within my soul, to fix this. I had to dig deep. My thoughts and my thought process would ultimately determine my destiny.

One thing gave me great strength during those days of rehab.

I drew upon that out of body experience that I felt while I lay unconscious in the hospital a few short days ago. When I thought about that, it filled me with a comfortable energy.

A lovely healing energy.

There is a reason why I've survived this. I had clarity like I could never have imagined before. Somehow, the noise and clutter of life had been swept away.

I'd been cleaned to my core, and granted a second opportunity.

BY THE FOURTH or fifth rehab session, I took matters into my own hands. I needed control. I might not have been ready for it, but I wanted it.

I started asking questions and demanding things of the cardiac team. I told them to speed up the treadmill.

They would often look at me in puzzlement and say things like, 'I don't think so Mickey. You aren't ready for it.

'We can speed it up next week."

My reply slowly began to sound familiar to them.

'Speed it up... I want you to speed it up now.'

If they didn't, I'd wait until they had their backs turned and then I switched it up a couple of notches without them seeing.

The speeds at that time started around 2.5, but I'd wait my moment to switch it up to 2.7. That set the target for next week... that's where I'd want to start.

My focus began to set a goal in terms of speed, one or two settings quicker than what the cardiac rehab team would set for me. That way, psychologically I knew I was ahead of the curve. If they set me up with a 0.5 incline, I would reset it at 1.5 incline.

There was a constant checking of my heart rate throughout.

I'd get caught on the odd occasion changing the settings. 'What's going on here, Mickey? Stick with the programme, Mickey.'

I'd ask them to check the monitor and tell them, 'If I'm okay, let's keep going'. I'd use quite a few of those little mind games to set goals for myself.

The treadmill that I used in the cardiac rehab centre was close to a floor-to-ceiling window that provided a panoramic view across the car park. I'd look left into the parking lot and see people coming in and out of the hospital, and think those people are coming here to get better.

Beyond that, was a lovely neat little row of homes with a range of coloured doors. Next, I'd look up at the sky and speak positively to myself… *I'm in control of this.*

A positive mindset is all about choices. I can choose to look at the bright blue sky and dream about getting out of this hospital as a new man, or I can look across to the right-hand side of those houses and see something different… Nyack graveyard.

I can't count the number of times that I got it tough on that treadmill, glanced across at the graveyard… and thought *No.*

No way.

Not yet.

Not for a long time yet.

Those were the little mind games that I used throughout rehab.

MY MINDSET REQUIRED goals.

Achievable goals… Goals that would challenge me.

While I was sitting at home browsing the internet and looking for some motivation, I stumbled across a guy called Dr Wayne Dyer. He had published a string of very popular books based around the psychology of self-improvement.

On Dyer's website, he's labelled 'The father of motivation'. His influence on me was phenomenal. Whenever you find yourself in a dark place, it's extraordinarily difficult to change your mindset. Even moving into a neutral space takes an incredible effort.

What I found out from Dyer is that every one of the thoughts that I would think resulted in an action. In other words, if I could find something to think about that inspired me, I would immediately start to live that thought.

You become the person that you are, as a result of what you think. If I thought that I was terribly sick, then I was 100% right. If I thought that I was making progress and I was going to get better, then I was also 100% correct.

During that early recovery and rehab phase, I consciously switched the positive filter on in my brain. I began to take the attitude that needed to affirm all the good things that were happening to get me back to where I needed to be. It was such a simple but incredibly effective thing to do.

Pre-heart attack, I would waken up at 5am and stare at the ceiling, and I'd spend those moments thinking about the 10 jobs that I'd running that day.

I'd be thinking about all of the men on those jobs and the pressure would begin to build. I'd be creating 100 different problems in my head. Who owed me money that day? Who did I owe money to that day? You name it.

Anything that I could think of that was negative; I spent those moments rolling them all around in my mind, all those negative thoughts, and not one of them was going to help me achieve one thing that day.

From the moment that my foot hit the bedroom floor, I was on the back foot. I was in a spiral to the bottom. I was in a completely reactive situation. I was chasing money, and I was chasing problems. I was chasing *everything*.

There was no level of inner contentment in my head, there was no inner peace. I'm a firm believer that negative mindset fed into my heart attack.

So what has changed?

EVERY MORNING, I wake up, I bless myself and I thank God that I am alive.

That's really all that matters. Once you wake up you are winning, I don't care who you are. Tomorrow is not guaranteed for anyone.

It's very difficult for people to understand that, unless you've been down that road yourself. What I do is face each day with complete gratitude. I'm completely grateful for what I have. I've two wonderful children and a beautiful wife… great family, great in-laws, great work and great friends.

I've so much to be grateful for.

It's often down to what we choose to see, that will ultimately determine how we live. If you wake up in the morning and you choose to see anger and hatred, then that's exactly what you are going to see.

That's your perception of the world, right there and then.

The sun is going to rise and set again every day. The rivers are going to continue to flow. Trees will blossom, and grass will grow. There's a real intelligence going on in the world that in the vast majority of cases we are not hard-wired to see.

We aren't choosing to see it.

I made the decision to see it.

My recovery starts with this.

BACK IN THE cardiac rehab, I'd move across from the treadmill to the rowing machine. I'd really push myself as hard as I could. I got myself into the mindset that this was the perfect place to do that.

I was in a hospital that had already saved my life. If I couldn't push myself here, then where could I?

I'd glance around the room to make sure that the rehab nurse wasn't watching me, and then I'd move the dial on the machine... up. They had a programme of recovery for me.

I wanted to go one better than their recovery plan.

One more notch, up all the time from where the cardiac rehab team wanted me to work at.

For me, always one more notch.

PART 5

The Jersey

THE 1998 TYRONE Senior Championship win with Ardboe gave me a belief that anything was possible.

The opportunity to prove that, came only a few short weeks later when I got the call up from Danny Ball to join the 1999 Tyrone senior football squad. I was thrilled to be asked.

When I walked into the dressing-rooms at Brackaville for the first training session, I was sitting close to Peter Canavan. Three years before, he was my teacher. But in Tyrone, he was legendary. Almost mythical.

You cannot begin to understand how people felt about this slight, small genius, who brought so much pleasure with the way he played football.

And here I was, sharing a dressing-room with him.

It wasn't only Canavan that I looked up to in that room. Ciaran 'Dinky' McBride from Omagh. Fay Devlin from my own club Ardboe. Paul Devlin, Chris Lawn and Stephen Lawn from the neighbouring club Moortown. Seamus McCallan and Ronan McGarrity from Carrickmore.

All these legends that played on the Tyrone team in the 1995 All-Ireland final and lost out by a single point, and a terrible refereeing decision to Dublin.

Looking back at that time, it is amazing how the preparation of the county sides has changed so much. As part of the build-up to the Ulster Championship, we went to Ballybofey in Donegal for a team bonding weekend two weeks ahead of the game.

I didn't drink at that time, but it was carnage. The lads were going buck mad through the hotel. We were up the street, in and out of every public house we could find.

It might have been more appropriate to call it a stag weekend.

But it was brilliant. Serious fun. When you had big Seamus McCallan and Canavan leading the charge, you knew that you were in for a serious night's craic. It was a year that will be remembered by the day that we played Down in Casement Park in the opening round of the Ulster Championship.

Before we went to the game that day, we were told to gather in Killyman for a warm-up. The weather could not have been better. For us it was boiling, somewhere in the mid 80s… 30 degrees. That didn't bother our coaches. They ran the s***e out of us in Killyman for over half an hour.

It was as if we had just played a championship match.

I ALWAYS TRAVELLED with Fay Devlin and Chris 'Cricko' Lawn. As we pulled off the M1 motorway to join the road into Anderstown where Casement Park was located, I turned to see Fay fast asleep in the car. He was exhausted.

The team was shattered taking the field that day.

Fay ended up marking the lightning-fast Mickey Linden that day, which was a tough task on the best of days. Down gave us a toasting. Ciaran McCabe kicked two goals and three points, and we were sent away with our tails between our legs. Wee James McCartan was on the line with a pair of crutches, which were meant to be supporting his weight, but spent most of the time in the air celebrating Down scores.

I didn't get a look-in that year in terms of game time, but I learnt so much from it. I'd managed to do something that few people every do. I'd got on to the Tyrone senior football squad before I'd even got on to the county under-21 squad.

That would happen later that year when Mickey Harte asked me onto his panel. That was my first interaction with Mickey. We got on really well at that point. Maybe that had something to do with the fact that myself, Mark Harte and Stephen O'Neill were the only men that didn't take a drink on the panel. We hugged the seats at the front of the bus, while all the lunatics took up the back seats.

I togged out at midfield alongside Cormac McAnallen in the opening round of the Ulster Championship campaign, a campaign that was short lived. Derry beat us in the opening round in Omagh. They had a quality team with the likes on Paul McFlynn, Johnny McBride and Fergal Doherty pulling the strings for them.

It was a devastating loss for us, because that team was comprised of a lot of players who had won All-Ireland minor medals with Tyrone the previous year. I was over-age for the team the following year and the players left on the panel would go on to dominate and win the next two Ulster under-21 and All-Ireland titles.

When I look back at that time, I really regret the fact that I didn't get a run with the Tyrone minors or under-18 team, prior to the under-21s and seniors. Mickey Harte didn't pick me for the 1997 and '98 minor panels.

That was my fault though, not his.

THE OPPORTUNITY CAME to stay with my uncle in America through the summer months. When I was 17 and 18 years of age, that's exactly what I did.

I jumped at that chance.

Little did I know then how much of an impact that country would have on me.

IN 2000 I'D find another opportunity to pull on a county jersey; this time for New York GAA in the opening round of the Connacht Senior Football Championship against Galway.

The game was played in Tuam, and I lined out at centre-forward, marking Ray Silke, who had lifted Sam Maguire just two seasons previously. I managed to score a point off him before Galway went on to win the game by 10 points.

I was flying at that point in terms of the football I was playing, and the fitness levels I had reached.

But I was making the wrong choices. Instead of just staying at home in Tyrone and keeping a low profile, I was bouncing about all over the place. Inevitably, I chose adventure over everything else.

Before I went back to the States, the Tyrone senior manager at the time, Eugene McKenna, called me. He wanted to know if I'd join the panel in 2001?

I chose America.

Another poor choice.

When I came back later in the fall, I concentrated all my efforts on being successful with the Ardboe team in the 2002 championship. That only lasted as far as May, when Killyclogher beat us in the opening round of the championship in Pomeroy.

As far as I was concerned, that was the season over.

Instead of going back to America, I grabbed my guitar and jumped on a plane and landed in Spain. I had a few contacts in that part of the world and I spent the summer season playing music in a bar in Santa Ponza with Colin Doherty.

It was madness.

One long party. One day barely separated from another.

Music and mayhem.

That year, I watched Tyrone win their first National League title, progress through Ulster and win another Anglo Celt Cup before they took on Sligo in the All-Ireland quarter-final. I wasn't in the best of form at that point because I knew that I'd made another poor choice not taking up Eugene's offer. Brian Robinson from Donaghmore played on that Tyrone team that day.

Robbo was a really good friend of mine on the under-21 team previously and he was one of the only players to come out of that game with any credibility. His performances that year saw him nominated for an All-Star award.

I sat in Durty Nelly's Bar in Santa Ponza and watched in total disbelief as Tyrone lost out to Sligo. More accurately, they were annihilated by Eamon O'Hara as he inspired Sligo. At the end of that game, I was miserable.

We were playing from 10pm to 2pm, night after night. While the money was brilliant, holidaymakers see every night as a Saturday night and they want to party… every night. They demanded and got a high-octane Irish music gig every single night. That takes enormous energy and the schedule was punishing.

My link to home was Internet Messenger thanks to an Internet Café down the street. Locked into a party atmosphere and the energy needed to sustain that, and wrecking my head thinking that I should be at home playing football. It was two entirely different worlds competing with each other.

Truth is, I loved both and wanted to do both. Truth also is, that you cannot play football without turning your back entirely on the music scene, with the late nights and lifestyle choices. Soon, it became apparent that Mickey Harte was set to become the next Tyrone manager. I knew then that I wanted to go home and make the 2003 team.

Mickey was appointed as expected later that year.

He hit the ground running by organising a series of trial matches before Christmas. I attended every trial game and then felt devastation as I wasn't asked onto the panel. I didn't make the cut.

I was gutted.

I couldn't get my head around why I hadn't made it. I felt that I put in a good performance in each of the try-out games. Harte called me himself; he told me that I'd missed out narrowly as he had to pick just 30 players.

On reflection, Mickey had a crop of new players coming in from successful under-21 teams but he also had a raft of experience in men like Peter Canavan, Chris Lawn, Gerard Cavlan, Brian Dooher and Collie Holmes. Those were serious footballers and household names in the GAA, not just in Tyrone, but in Ulster and Ireland. I'd a strong feeling that squad were going to do something special.

If I wanted to switch off and forget about gaelic football, I couldn't. At the time I was working for *Teamtalk* magazine, which was a glossy magazine reporting on everything about the GAA in Tyrone.

I had serious craic writing the odd article and selling advertising space, working alongside GAA nut cases, Kenny and Chris Curran, who owned the business at the time. The current owners of the online business, Kevin Kelly and Noel McGinn would drop in with articles and stories about matches and skirmishes from games all over the place. The craic was good, and the working day flew by in that office.

My evenings provided an opportunity to get away from it and, around that time, I spent a bit of time fishing on Lough Neagh with my cousin, Ned Sheehy. All the time, my mind was fixed on getting better to make the next Tyrone panel. I'd redoubled my effort to play well with Ardboe. I thought that would be me in the 2004 panel.

Not for the first time about football, I would be wrong.

A FEW LADS from home and I decided that we would go down to Roscommon to take in Tyrone's first National League game of the 2003 season.

It was to be Mickey Harte's first game in charge. If I couldn't play, I could still cheer from the stands. On the Friday night before the game on Sunday, I visited my aunt Josie's house in Ardboe with a cousin of mine, Bella Campbell.

Josie was a sister of my uncle, Jim Curran. Jim had been part of Mickey Harte's backroom team throughout his stint as Tyrone minor and under-21 manager. Jim was the logistics man, taking care of booking transport and organising meals.

That evening, Jim called my house looking for me. Somebody at home told him to ring Josie. When he got me, he sounded urgent… 'Mickey, you've to give Mickey Harte a call. He's looking to speak to you'.

I knew immediately what it meant.

'Is this true?

'Is this man looking me… for Tyrone?

'Did someone get injured?'

Jim's voice brought me back down to earth. He gave me a number to call and he gave away nothing. He probably knew, but he said nothing. I moved into an empty room in the house and started to dial the number.

I could hear by the commotion at the door that I had an audience with their ears pressed against the door. This was a big deal. This was how serious we took our football in this part of the world; this meant something to everyone down our way.

Mickey came onto the phone in the calmest of voices.

'Yes Mickey, how are you?'

'Listen, one or two men have had to drop out this weekend with injuries. Would you be interested in coming in with us for the foreseeable future?'

I was about to burst open with joy, but I was trying to stay as calm as possible. I responded, 'Absolutely Mickey, I'd be delighted to come on board. Absolutely.'

How did I get the words out without screaming with joy?

Harte replied, 'That's great, I'll get your gear sent down with Jim and we will see you on Sunday morning in Quinn's Corner.'

That house was bedlam that evening. It was so memorable. I'd made it into this special panel of players.

The panel met early on the Sunday morning at 'Quinn's Corner' on the Ballygawley line between Dungannon and Ballygawley. Paudge Quinn owned the bar and restaurant there. He was the last man to score a goal for Tyrone in an All-Ireland final, in 1986.

Quinn's Corner was a GAA bar and restaurant owned by a GAA legend in that part of the world, and it was exactly the place that a Tyrone senior team would gather before going off to a game.

I remember sitting in a circle of chairs in the middle of the floor in Quinn's Corner and Mickey Harte meticulously going through the notes that he had written down before addressing us.

He shared with us exactly how he wanted to play the game. I kept thinking to myself, 'Am I validated to be here? Should I be here?'

I was so grateful to be in that circle, and now I wanted to push on and be not just in the squad of players, but on the starting team. I wanted to prove a point that I'm here on merit.

I know that some people would say I got on the panel because of Jim Curran, but believe me, Jim was one of my harshest critics. He didn't miss me when he thought that I wasn't pulling my weight or playing well.

It was Mickey's first game in charge, and we lost it to a very hungry Roscommon team. I didn't play that day, but my chance would come. I wasn't the only one called into the panel. Some players came in and were let go again shortly after that. Some players returned from injury, but I kept the head down and worked like a dog every Tuesday and Thursday night.

I was just waiting for the tap on the shoulder to let me know that I was next to be offloaded. The weeks passed without incident.

I GOT MY first game for Tyrone in the McKenna Cup final against Monaghan in Brewster Park.

I lined out alongside Seamus McCallan at midfield.

It would prove to be the last match that Seamus would play for Tyrone. After that game he told Mickey that he felt that he couldn't contribute any more to the Tyrone cause, and left the panel.

I'd say he's questioned that decision in his own head, ever since.

A FEW DAYS after that, the Championship panel was announced, and I made the cut this time.

I got another run-out against Galway in the league, played in Pomeroy. I came on early as a sub and we won by five points. One thing struck me when I was on the pitch that day, and it surprised me because I had been in the dressing-room and training matches.

But then you look around you and see all these players in Tyrone jerseys. Brian McGuigan's talent was obvious to me for a long time, but then add in Stephen O'Neill, Chris Lawn, Frank McGuigan junior. I felt that day, I was justified in being there.

Some people will know the characters associated with that squad were famed for their devilment. The trips to and from our training sessions were legendary. In our car, my uncle Jim was driving myself, Brian and Frank McGuigan, and Gavin Devlin. Occasionally, Owen 'Mugsy' Mulligan would join us.

The first point of order was getting the radio tuned to the local station, Q101.

As players were making their way back to university, they would send a barrage of texts to the poor DJ who would read out all this innuendo, and he seemed to have no filter whatsoever.

Some lessons were learned the hard way. One morning we boarded the bus in Ballygawley and I was flush with £250 in my pocket after a good week's work.

Off I went to the back of the bus, to the card school. Down there, certain veterans had their place... Peter Canavan, Kevin 'Hub' Hughes, Gavin Devlin, Ryan McMenamin, Brian McGuigan and Gerard Cavlan.

Little did I know, I was walking into the Lion's Den.

We were playing 'Chase the Ace' but the whole thing was rigged.

We stopped in Castleblaney after an hour for something to eat. I hadn't a penny left. I was destroyed. They were ruthless. I was cross, but I soon learned my lesson. When we got out at Castleblaney, Canavan got up from his seat and the ace of hearts was stuck to his backside. And there was me asking Mugsy for the lend of a fiver, so I could buy myself an ice cream.

Mealtimes were another time to be watchful. No matter how much you needed to go to the toilet, you didn't get up. If you left, you'd come back to the entire contents of the salt shaker in your soup. Maybe the salt shaker as well.

At the end of a meal one other day, I went into a toilet cubicle. I heard the door beside me opening and a sixth sense kicked in. I stood up and got tight to the door, only to see a tsunami of water being emptied over the top of my head. I got off lightly that day. Mugsy had orchestrated it but his shooting accuracy let him down on that occasion.

Paddy Tally came on board in 2003 to train Tyrone. Hardly anyone outside of hardcore Tyrone football people were aware of him. I'd played senior club football against him the previous year, when he was playing for Galbally.

For some reason, I loved playing against Galbally. Especially up there. If there was a team in Tyrone that was similar to Ardboe, it was them. Like ourselves, they were severely impacted by The Troubles. I just felt that there was a similarity there. They were hard and tough, and they cared about the game.

I was one of the fitter players in the squad and I'd always have put a lot of effort into my training. But I only thought I was fit. I remember Paddy taking his first training session in Edendork. Immediately, I knew this was a whole different level.

You required a whole different level of thinking. There were no excuses. Get it done. Don't question it.

Tally knew exactly what he was doing. The complexity of the drills was testament to that; there were never any static drills. Everything had a purpose, everything could be integrated into a game.

The drills were dynamic, and they made you think. There was a real cutting edge and innovative game-based context to what we were being asked to do. You could see exactly how those drills would play out in a match. You always knew at the time of a training session that you were going to be busted, but you always looked forward to the session.

There were tackle bags everywhere.

I'd never seen tackle bags on a GAA pitch before. That resulted in hard hits flying around everywhere from all directions. At times, it felt there were a dozen people clawing at you, with all the hits. And the noise and aggression.

TACKLE!

TACKLE! TACKLE!

Mickey and Paddy had devised a plan.

Paddy's job was to instil it into us on the training field. We didn't know it at the time, but that level of intensity on the training field was all about getting ready for Kerry and All-Ireland champions, Armagh somewhere down the line.

Harte stood back and let Tally at it, but he observed everything that was going on.

He was cooking up a plan. And, I was in the mix. I couldn't have been happier; I couldn't have been more excited at where this was bringing us.

THE TRAINING WAS at an intensity and level that I've never experienced before or seen since. I remember standing in to mark Conor Gormley and thinking, *I'm going well here.* We did a fitness test early in the year and I came on out top, followed by Sean Cavanagh and Brian McGuigan.

The in-house games were immense. They were tough, fast and everyone around you seemed to be flying. The week after the drawn game with Down in the Ulster final we took part in another in-house game in Dunmoyle, home to Errigal Ciaran.

I was told to line out at full-forward where I was expecting to go in against Chris Lawn. It turned out to be Cormac McAnallen.

Mickey Harte had decided that Cormac needed to switch from midfield in the drawn game to full-back for the replay. I stood in there watching Peter Canavan and Owen Mulligan putting on an exhibition at the other end of the field, while the wizard that was Brian McGuigan was spraying balls into them. It was incredible. I felt sorry for Cricko and Mickey McGee trying to mark them. Their pace, movement and accuracy were mesmerising.

All the time, I had fingertips constantly on my back. It was like a grizzly bear breathing down my left ear. Cormac McAnallen was fully focused and in game mode; you just weren't going to get an inch from him. When Cormac committed, he was fully engaged. One hundred percent or nothing for him. If he needed to take man and ball at the same time, then no problem.

I MADE MY championship debut against Down in the Ulster Championship final replay. I recall sitting in the stand and getting a shout down to get ready to go.

The first thought that went through my head was, *Right! This is it.* I had a serious bit of pride in representing all the coaches that had stuck with me and told me that I was good enough. This was all for them, and I felt a flood of emotion.

I came on during the second-half for fellow club man Brian McGuigan. Harte told me that I was going into centre-forward. His final words were, 'Now is your chance... SHINE!'

The game was over as a contest by the time I came on, but do you think I cared? It was a complete thrill to get a run out on the Clones turf on Ulster final day and the ground jammed to the rafters. It was great to get out there and open up the legs. Wearing a Tyrone jersey in an Ulster final.

The stuff of dreams. I contested a couple of kickouts with Down's Dan Gordon and played a couple of one-twos with Frank McGuigan. Thinking even at that point that I was there. In the fray.

Where I had always wanted to be.

TO SOME, IT mightn't look like or feel like much. But I came from a place in Tyrone where football was everything. Almost all that was ever talked about. People slept, ate and breathed it every day of the week.

During The Troubles, in our part of the world football was our bread and water. I knew that I was a fringe player in 2003 but I was pushing as hard as I could to make a positive impact on the squad.

The Ulster final celebrations lasted only a short time. Gerard Cavlan had a bar in Dungannon at the time and we went there for the Sunday night. But only that night. There was a feeling amongst the players that there was more in this team, so the focus returned very quickly to working hard again.

Monday night was recovery night, followed by another tough session on the Tuesday night. People will always see the footballing geniuses that played on that 2003 team, but few ever got to see the camaraderie and the sense of brotherhood. That squad had a unique bond.

They could party hard on a Sunday night and be back cutting lumps out of each other the following evening in an in-house match. There was no bullshit. We were all going to have the craic along the way, but there was a job to be done.

My roommate that year was Sean Cavanagh and we got on like a dream.

Earlier in the year we played Donegal on a foggy day up in Coalisland in a

National League game. Gavin 'Horse' Devlin had a great game that day, playing centre-back, but we were struggling badly in the first-half.

When we came into the changing rooms at half-time, Mickey Harte wasn't a happy man. It was the first and only time that I saw Harte lose the head. I mean he really lost the head. The water bottles were kicked off the ceiling in Coalisland that day.

His words will never leave me.

'I can deal with a lot of s**t, but I can't deal with a lack of effort.' The changing room was silent. That moment was the turning point in Tyrone's year. Sean Cavanagh was switched from full-forward to midfield, and he excelled as we went on to draw level with and then beat Donegal in the second-half. Cavanagh put on an exhibition in the middle of the field, and Sean Cavanagh's career changed from that day forward.

He was an animal to share a room with. I would wake up in the morning and see him down on the floor doing press-ups.

I'd be lying in bed laughing at him, asking, 'What's wrong with you? You're not wise, man.'

He did everything by the book and had a lovely routine of polishing his football boots the night before a game, setting them on the windowsill to dry.

We were given a green formula; a kind of protein shake that most tried and few stuck with it. It was so rough... you wouldn't give it to a donkey. Cavanagh could hold his nose and sink it, while I'd be close to vomiting when the smell would hit my nose.

Sean Cavanagh was destined to be one of the greatest players of all time. He was all-in from day one, at only 19 years of age. Complete commitment, like I'd never seen. He was only a youngster, but by God he was passionate. He'd finish that year with an All Star award and Young Player of the Year award.

It happened, because he made it happen.

IT WAS EASY to admire the superstars on our team, and they were everywhere, but I identified with the other players on the squad who, like me, had to fight for game time.

Seamus Mulgrew from Donaghmore really had his life together. He was a different type of character from the big personalities in the squad. His own man, and yet everything you'd want in a teammate… committed, working his backside off at training, and one of the less heralded names.

Seamus was studying to be a doctor at the time, and he always carried himself well. He didn't care what anyone thought of him, just quietly went about his business. His late father, John Mulgrew was a key man in Club Tyrone, the fundraising body for Tyrone GAA, and from subsequent conversations with John I could see how Seamus was cast from the same mould as John.

In terms of conducting yourself, I was constantly amazed at Kevin 'Hub' Hughes. He was an inspiration to all of us. Kevin and his family suffered some dark, dark days while he played for Tyrone. In 1997 his brother, Paul died in a road traffic accident on the Ballygawley line close to his home. He was just 22.

Four years later his sister, Helen was killed in another car accident on the same stretch of road. Hub Hughes was a mountain of resilience. You cannot imagine the suffering and pain associated with losing two siblings at such a young age.

He was impeccable. How could he even think about playing football? Every day he togged out for Tyrone and crossed the white line, he performed. For us, they were small snippets of life that you recall from time to time, but for Hub, it was all his life.

Everybody gets tested at some point.

Nobody escapes it, but some people get more than their fair share. He carried it on his shoulders with grace and humility.

POST-MATCH ANALYSIS took place in Myles McCann's restaurant in Omagh. We would go upstairs, and Mickey would dissect the game.

Peter Canavan was captain and he demanded full attention to all that work. Everyone listened when he spoke. I can still see him at training, standing at a cone in the middle of a session almost squealing to get a breath, or at times bent over in two... sucking at an inhaler.

Despite his asthma, when the whistle went for the next man in, he was gone. Even thinking of it now, *Jesus Christ of Almighty*. I mean, he took off like a bullet leaving a gun. It was a whole different kind of mindset.

I carry memories like that with me every day.

They spill over into life, business, and sport. Mind over matter. Those moments fill the foundations of my life.

My stand out moment regarding Canavan revolves around the 2003 All-Ireland semi-final at half-time. Peter went off in the first-half with an ankle injury. Tyrone were flying. Every tackling drill that Paddy Tally had put us through and every ounce of sweat that we poured out on those training fields was coming to fruition that day. Kerry were rocked back and they had no answer to us.

Canavan entered the circle of players in the changing rooms at half-time that day knowing that we were just 35 to 40 minutes away from reaching an All-Ireland final.

As he hopped on one leg, the tears were running down his face. He told us that he had never asked anyone to do anything out there that he couldn't do himself. He was asking us to go out and do this one thing for him now. Get over the line and get into an All-Ireland final.

The tears started flowing from players in the circle straight after that. This was the only time that Peter Canavan ever asked anyone to do anything for him.

By God, it was going to get done.

Nothing else had to be said. There wasn't another word before the players walked out that changing room door, turned the corner into the tunnel... and ran out onto the pitch.

Two weeks prior to the All-Ireland final, Paddy Tally handed us a blank sheet of paper at the end of a training session in Omagh. He instructed us to go home and write one good comment about everyone on the squad, except yourself.

'Write down why they are on this team.'

We were asked to have it back into him within a week. The night before the All-Ireland final, we were in the hotel at Killiney Castle in Dublin. When we completed our team meeting, Mickey Harte held up a small piece of paper and passed it around the circle.

That piece of paper was about the size of my thumb. He asked us if it bothered us? We looked around, confused and he told us that the snippet of paper was the average height difference between Armagh and Tyrone players.

He asked us if it bothered us?

Next, he passed around a pound of sugar.

Same question. Does that bother you?

That's how much heavier on average the Armagh team are. In our minds, the difference was marginal and that left us ready to go.

We left to go back to our rooms after that. When we got to them, there was an envelope sitting on our pillow. There were three items in the envelope.

Rosary beads.

A miraculous medal.

A note with 29 comments explaining why Mickey Coleman was here!

Twenty-nine anonymous comments and reasons.

When I had finished reading it, I turned to Sean Cavanagh and I said, 'We are not getting beat tomorrow. We are not going to lose this f***ing game.'

Shortly after the Ulster final, Mickey had tasked me and his daughter, Michaela to teach the boys the Irish National Anthem… *Amhrán na bhFiann.*

Michaela was a beautiful and kind young woman, who in January 2010, whilst on honeymoon, was cruelly murdered in her hotel bedroom in Mauritius. Those who carried out that violent and cowardly act remain at large and her loss is still felt very deeply by her family, friends and those of us who knew her.

Michaela and I spent many nights going over the words with the rest of the players and every one of them took it very seriously. The anthem became part of us, part of our identity. Part of the fabric of who we are.

Despite all the things that had been said in a funny way, there was a real serious element to this. It was mentioned in Peter Canavan's speech after the All-

Ireland final. The press scoffed that Tyrone were like the British army… claiming we had no power in the south.

Whether people liked it or didn't like it, the players in Tyrone at that time couldn't care less. This is what they were about.

Our Nationalism, and for some, our Republicanism, was part of us and we apologised to no one for that.

On our way home from the All-Ireland final, Peter Canavan got the bus to stop at the spot where Aidan McAnespie was shot dead by the British armed forces. Aidan was a GAA man, and a Tyrone man, killed because he cared enough about our game that he would walk through and beyond a British army checkpoint close to the border to the Aghaloo O'Neills GAA ground.

Peter did that because it was the right thing to do.

On the bus on the way into Croke Park that morning, Mickey called me up to the front of the bus and I led the lads in a rendition of *Amhrán na bhFiann*. We got stuck on the route in and we sang it another couple of times.

We were really passionate about singing it. I'd later use the same tactic with the New York Feile team in 2017 to give them a sense of their place and their identity in Irish American heritage.

As I sat there in that changing room ahead of the game, I was filled with a great sense of pride that we had made it this far. All Ireland football final day is as big as it gets in Ireland. There's an increased rhythm to it that sweeps up everyone who has any interest in the GAA.

It's our Super Bowl Sunday.

PULSE

THE TEAM HAD been named earlier in the week and I knew that I wasn't close to the starting line-up. Nonetheless, there's always an anticipation that maybe, just maybe I'd get some game time. The scenarios were always running through my head.

For now, I was deep underneath the Hogan Stand in Croke Park. Eighty-two thousand people gathered in anticipation just a few metres above our heads.

For now, all I could do was wait.

You get used to waiting. As a member of the substitutes and wider playing panel, you get used to it. You try not to. When you begin to accept your position as just a panel member you are finished. I looked around and spotted another 14 or 15 faces that might as well have been mirror images of me.

Waiting for their opportunity.

The anticipation of what might happen. Their thoughts the same as mine. Will I get my chance?

Keep calm and focused... and wait.

Breathe. Be Ready.

Not excited... calm, prepared... prepared for the mayhem.

Ready to walk into a war.

Be ready.

I WAS CONFIDENT that the players who were starting could deliver. The run up to the final had been superb. There was a razor like sharpness and focus to everything that Mickey Harte and Paddy Tally had delivered.

The waiting in that dressing-room gave me time to think. In a few minutes, I'd be running out onto that Croke Park pitch and everyone that was close to me would be there in the stands. My mother and father, brothers and sisters, friends, and Tyrone supporters. That sense of anticipation that I got in that quiet time will live with me forever.

Next, the quiet words of encouragement. It was the role of the substitutes to get in and around the starting team and offer them the final words of support. Yes, we wanted their starting jersey, but we wanted the collective to win more than anything else.

The noise levels increased in the warm-up area under the stand, as did the heart rate level. More noise at the door to the corridor into the tunnel as I took my place in the line of substitutes and formed a wall of support around each player as the left to go to war.

Led by Peter Canavan.

The man that I'd crossed paths with as a student. Now he was my teammate and our captain on the biggest day of them all.

Oh My God! What the hell is this?

I turned the corner from the corridor into the sunlight, and it hit me.

Thunderous noise.

Horns, music, drums.

People everywhere. Energy filled every sinew and tissue in my body... 82,400 people, the place was bouncing. I sprinted across the field to join the team for the photo close to the vast Cusack Stand.

We had talked about this beforehand. When we broke from the photo, we would sprint to our positions for the warm-up. We had intent and we needed to show that.

I wasn't even starting, and I was grinding the gumshield with my teeth. Canavan marched us down to the Hill 16 end of the ground for the warm-up, the area Armagh were already using for *their* warm-up.

All hell broke loose.

I remember Horse Devlin giving the rallying call to get wired into the Armagh men. It was a sea of heavy shoulders, and you could hear the welts and slaps of contact all around the place.

There was that much energy around the place, that I think I may have even smacked into some of my own players.

Myself and another one of the substitutes, Frank McGuigan, used to set ourselves a target of seeing how many points the two of us could kick in the warm-up. I was queuing up to take a kick at one stage and was lifted into the air and knocked sidewards. It was crazy stuff.

All this and the first whistle to start the game hadn't even been blown.

ANOTHER SEA OF calm.

Our changing room at half-time that day was surely amongst the calmest places in the country. Harte brought that calmness.

Everything was well thought out.

Everything was run with meticulous precision.

On a day like that it would have been very easy to get caught up in the moment and lose focus on exactly what all of this was about.

Mickey Harte was solid. He had explained multiple times prior to this that we were in control of the controllables. The emotion in a dressing-room at half-time was *controllable*.

Clear and simple instructions. We took it all on board. I processed the parts of it that I felt impacted on me the most. if I got an opportunity.

I remained calm and waited.

JESUS!

THIS MIGHT happen. This might actually happen.

By that point we were a little bit of a mess. The game had entered injury time.

Our calm persona as patient substitutes was replaced by nerves and pleas to the referee to blow the final whistle.

All protocol about sitting in the substitutes area in the stand was dispensed with. We were now hugging the side line and praying for the final whistle. Waiting, as our hearts thumped through our chests.

Waiting, as our hearts thumped through our chests.

Agonisingly, the play out on the field rolled on and on.

Then it came.

The wait was over. Out of the midst of the cacophony of noise and bedlam, came a shrill blast of one long whistle.

I know it was followed by two more, but I heard nothing.

Noise and bodies crashed into us from all directions. We were completely overcome by a sea of people from all sides.

We did it.

Tyrone senior footballers had delivered. The Sam Maguire Cup was coming to the Red Hand County for the first time ever. Thousands and thousands and thousands of people everywhere. and years and years of torture put to rest.

Tyrone people all over Croke Park. All over County Tyrone. All around the globe.

The wait was over.

I attempted to make my way out onto the field to throw my arms around my teammates, but it was impossible. Tyrone men, women and children were flooding onto the field.

I was hoisted onto the shoulders of supporters. I didn't play a single second, but it didn't matter. We were all treated the same. All I could see was an ocean of people and then, out across the pitch, player after player on the shoulders of supporter moving slowly back to the tunnel in front of the Hogan Stand.

THE DRESSING-ROOM was simply crazy.

I'm still not sure how so many people ended up in there. Family members. Members of the county board. Photographers. TV crews.

Madness. Just a beautiful madness, and so many treasured memories.

Not least the photo of all the players from Ardboe with the Sam Maguire Cup.

It's one of my most treasured possessions. A photo with the greatest prize in our sport and the men that I'd grown up with. Four Ardboe footballers... Gavin Devlin, Frank McGuigan, Brian McGuigan and myself, alongside another Ardboe man, my uncle Jim.

Jim, who looked after all of the logistics for the senior footballers, while Mickey Harte was in charge.

The bus trip out to the Citywest Hotel afterwards was another incredible sight. TV cameras on the bus. People hanging out of cars driving around the bus, and then another wave of hundreds and hundreds of fans at the hotel.

I only slept for about one hour that night.

THE NEXT MORNING, I got a knock on my hotel room door.

When I opened the door, Cormac McAnallen, our full-back on the team, was standing with a very broad smile on his face.

He came into my room waving a newspaper.

Front page.

Main picture.

There was Cormac, fists clenched and arms out wide.

'Look Mickey, we've won the All Ireland! We've won the All Ireland.'

I gave him the tightest hug in the world.

We were in heaven.

PART **6**

Brantry Boy

Dr McKenna Cup final 2004
Tyrone 1-22 Donegal 0-7

Tyrone annihilated Donegal in the Dr McKenna Cup final at MacCumhaill Park, Ballybofey, yesterday.

The reigning All-Ireland champions lost last year's final of this competition to Monaghan but it seems that manager Mickey Harte's promise to treat every game and competition with the same importance is a warning to any team hoping to relieve them of their league and championship titles.

Tyrone team: John Devine; Ryan McMenamin, Cormac McAnallen (Captain), Ciaran Gourley; Conor Gormley, Gavin Devlin, Philip Jordan (0-1); Kevin Hughes (0-3), Sean Cavanagh (0-2); Brian Dooher (0-1), Brian McGuigan (1-0), Gerard Cavlan (0-5, two frees); Mark Harte (0-6, five frees), Leo Meehan (0-1), Enda McGinley (0-1). Subs: Joe McMahon for Jordan; Barry Collins (0-1) for Dooher; Brendan Donnelly for Gormley; Shane Sweeney for McMenamin; Mickey Coleman (0-1) for McGinley.

(*The Irish Times*, Monday, February 23, 2004)

I WAS GUTTED not to be starting.

Mickey Harte had named the team on the Thursday evening after training, and I wasn't in.

The 2004 Dr McKenna Cup final was huge for us. If we could win this game, we would complete the full set. For the first time in our history, Tyrone GAA would hold every single trophy possible for the county to win at senior football level.

The previous April we had won the National Football League title. Three months later we had added the Ulster senior crown, and in September we annexed the holy grail of the Sam Maguire Cup and the All-Ireland Senior Football Championship.

It was a cold Sunday afternoon at the end of February.

For many people, this was only a pre-season competition that didn't mean very much. Not for us. We were going to Ballybofey in Donegal to take the Dr McKenna Cup trophy home. A final played against Donegal in Donegal's home ground.

It meant everything to us.

We had to win.

I'd made the starting team in two of the group games, against Derry in Omagh and Antrim in Casement Park. I was very happy with my form. I'd kicked a point from play in both of those games, and I felt like I was contributing very well.

I'd just have to stay calm, take my place on the bench and hope for the best. In the days prior to the start of the Dr McKenna Cup, Mickey told us that the captaincy of the team was changing. By 2004, Peter Canavan was fast approaching the end of his career. There would be at least another couple of seasons in him, but he was no longer going to be playing every game. Between him and Harte, they'd felt a fresh voice was required. The players were asked to cast a vote for his replacement. For the vast majority of us, there was only one man.

Cormac McAnallen from Eglish.

Cormac was quite simply the most dedicated player that I'd ever had the pleasure of playing with. He was driven by perfection. His brother, Donal would articulate that in the beautiful book that he would later write about Cormac, *The Pursuit of Perfection*.

Cormac's first final as Tyrone senior football captain was to be that Dr McKenna Cup final on Sunday, February 22, 2004. Many Ulster counties treated the Dr McKenna Cup competition as a pre-season warm-up and just a bit of a loosener ahead of the more serious league and championship later in the year.

That was never our style.

Mickey made it clear when he took over the management that he wanted to win every game. It didn't matter who the opposition were or what the competition was, Mickey wanted to win.

Cormac operated with a similar attitude.

He prepared for every game like it was an All-Ireland final. The Dr McKenna Cup final was the next game to win. That's all the mattered. In the dressing rooms in Ballybofey before the game he gave a speech that set the tone for the day.

We went out and destroyed Donegal.

By half-time we led by 10 points. Brian McGuigan had struck a goal from 30 yards out. At one stage in the second-half, we stretched the lead to 17 points.

We were a treat to watch.

We just wanted to win, and no one personified that more that the man wearing the No 3 and playing at full-back... Cormac.

I got my chance and ran onto the field as a substitute in the second-half. I replaced Enda McGinley and I managed to score a point. That was three games and three points for me in the Dr McKenna Cup that year, and I was happy enough with that contribution.

The one thing that struck me most about that day was the trophy presentation. I'd witnessed a couple of McKenna Cup trophy presentations in the years prior to that and they weren't the most exciting events in the world.

Nine times out of 10, the winning captain would collect the cup from the Ulster GAA president and almost reluctantly, and half-heartedly, hold it up with one hand.

Not Cormac. Not that day.

Cormac collected the trophy in both hands and quickly raised it up above his head. He held it there with the widest and cheesiest smile on his face. I remember feeling so proud to be part of a group of players that treated every opportunity with such addictive and positive energy. These guys were born winners. All they wanted to do was win. Mickey had replaced Peter Canavan with a man that wanted to win just as much as Peter and Mickey.

I was overwhelmed with how genuinely thrilled Cormac was to be holding that trophy above his head.

He had delivered at the first available opportunity as captain of Tyrone. He had led his county to more silverware, and he was a very happy man. With a captain like Cormac McAnallen to lead us, surely there was going to be more and more silverware to come.

NINE DAYS LATER.
At just 24 years of age...
Cormac would be dead.

Morning has broken, and I hear the news
Phones they are ringing, there's people confused
There's news that in Eglish. near the village of Moy
The angels have taken the Brantry Boy

My heart it is breaking, as I stand on the shore
For a friend and a leader, we will see you no more
Close to your home where the trout feed on fly
On this dull March morning, I ask myself, why?

The lake it is silent, the water is calm
There's no fishing boats, and there is no fisherman.
The Brantry is quiet, in the heart of Tyrone.
For a captain, a hero, a legend has gone.

(*The Brantry Boy*, by Mickey Coleman)

Tuesday, March 2, 2004

TYRONE WERE STILL the reigning All Ireland champions and with that title comes the most sought-after prize in gaelic county football… the Sam Maguire Cup.

Since we brought it back up the road the previous September, it had made its' way into countless houses, halls, schools, and dinner dances.

Tasked with being the custodian of the cup was Cuthbert Donnelly, a wonderfully warm man, and a former county chairman. He tirelessly brought it everywhere, spreading the magic to schools, hospitals, weddings, and care homes.

Wherever he went, he had a couple of rules. 'Sam' was treated with the utmost of respect, and no alcohol went into the chalice. As members of the panel, we were all afforded the honour of taking our turn to look after the biggest prize in our game.

My turn to look after the cup came on Monday, March 1, 2004. I'd been given the clear and strict instructions where it was to be brought the next morning when I'd finished with it. I was mindful of the fact that not everyone would have had the opportunity to leave their home and go out and see the trophy.

I wanted to concentrate on visiting those people first.

I called in Tommy McKenna's house down in Moortown and Sean Muldoon's house in Ardboe, and went from there.

I was in a relationship with a girl from Eglish at the time and I had planned on visiting the Daly family at their home in Eglish that Monday night. Before I left the house, I rang Cormac McAnallen's mobile.

There was no answer.

I now know that Cormac was in the gym in Armagh that night doing a session. That's why he didn't answer the phone. I stayed up in Eglish that evening with the Daly family.

I WAS USED to the mobile phone going off early in the morning, but this wasn't the sound of an alarm.

It was a phone call.

The name 'Jim' lit up the screen.

Uncle Jim?

Something felt strange about that.

The man never called me at that time of the morning.

What the hell time was it anyway? I checked the phone.

5:47am.

I answered and heard Jim say, 'Mickey... Cormac has passed away'.

I lay there motionless.

Cormac who?

'I can't believe it either Mickey... Cormac McAnallen is dead.'

How? Why?

What the hell is going on?

I just couldn't take in what I was hearing. It couldn't be Cormac McAnallen. The man was a machine. *Jesus no way.*

It couldn't be Cormac.

He's only 24.

I GOT OFF the phone.

The room was in darkness. I put on the beside locker light and there sitting right beside me was the Sam Maguire Cup. *How could this be?* I was in complete disbelief. I didn't know how to feel.

I was just numb with shock.

I was less than two miles away from Cormac McAnallen's house. *Should I get into the car and go there?*

The phone went off again. This time it was Paddy Tally. I can't even recall what we said to each other. A phone call filled with long periods of silence. *What was there to say? How could this be?*

I lifted the mobile phone again and rang my uncle Jim again.

We agreed that I should take the trophy over to Aughnacloy and drop it off with Cuthbert. I left the Daly house around 8:15am. The plan was to drive down through Eglish and take the road to Aughnacloy.

Just a short distance down the road is a local beauty spot called Brantry Lough, only a few hundred yards from Cormac's home.

I pulled the car into the car park and got out. I found myself drawn towards the small jetty that was positioned close to the car park.

I'd so wanted to drive the car down to Cormac's house and speak to his family, but I hadn't the courage to do so. I just stood there staring out into the lough, trying to gather my thoughts.

What is actually happening here?

That's when the first words came to me.

The lake it is silent,
the water is calm.
there is no fishing boats,
and there is no fisherman.

PULSE

IT FELT LIKE the whole world had stopped still. Right there at that moment I could hear nothing. I was enveloped in complete silence.

It filled every sense that I had.

Here I stood in a place deep in the heart of County Tyrone and all I could think about was the tragedy that was unfolding just a few yards up the road from me.

The adrenaline of shock and needing to get onto a phone to make and receive call after call had left me. The pace of the early morning hyperactivity was replaced by stillness.

Calmness.

I was completely dissolved into my surroundings.

Still and calm.

Silence.

Just silence.

Beautiful, tranquil... silence.

I GOT A phone call sometime around lunchtime that day, to say that Mickey Harte had called a players' meeting for everyone in Quinn's Corner for later that evening.

Like with so many journeys to training and matches, Jim Curran organised to collect myself, Brian McGuigan and Gavin Devlin. This car journey was very different from those before. Unlike those other journeys, we hardly spoke a word to each other.

When we reached Quinn's Corner, we had a private room, the silence broken only by the sound of men sobbing. Grown men in prime physical fitness, playing one of the most physical sports on the planet, in tears.

Broken by the loss of our friend. Our leader.

A humbling environment.

MICKEY ADDRESSED US first.

I don't remember too much of what he said at that time. I do recall what the next man to address us had to say... Kevin 'Hub' Hughes.

The previous September, he showed his character in winning the Man of the Match Award in the All-Ireland final.

He had also played on the same Tyrone minor team as Paul McGirr. Paul was just 17 years of age when he lost his life in the hours following a collision with an Armagh player in the 1997 Ulster Minor Championship in Healy Park.

Somehow, the players on that 1997 panel found the inner determination and resolve within themselves to go on and win the Ulster Minor Championship that year.

A few weeks after the Ulster decider, the team were five points down in the All-Ireland semi-final against Kerry. They fought back from that deficit to force a replay.

In the days between the two games, tragedy struck the Hughes family.

Kevin's older brother, Paul was just 22 years old when he was killed in a car crash not far from his own home. Kevin was only 18 when it happened. He and his family buried Paul on the Tuesday before the replay.

More tragedy was to follow. Four years later his sister, Helen would be killed in another car crash, on the same stretch of road, just 500 yards from where Paul had died. Unimaginable suffering for someone so young.

In the space of just four years, Kevin Hughes had lost his teammate, Paul McGirr, his brother, Paul and his sister, Helen.

There couldn't have been anyone better equipped to talk about dealing with the kind of adversity that Cormac's friends, and especially his family, were now feeling.

KEVIN, STANDING THERE in front of us, was so strong in that moment.

He didn't mince his words, saying, 'This has happened to poor Cormac. It's going to be painful.

'We are going to get past this.

'We need to be strong."

A few days later, the squad of players, background team and management team would form a guard of honour at Cormac's funeral in Eglish.

I've never witnessed anything like it before or since.

Thousands of people lined the roads and gathered around the chapel and graveyard to pay their final respects. The entire Tyrone senior football team and backroom staff formed a guard of honour alongside the funeral cortege.

We weren't on our own.

The entire Armagh panel and management team joined us. Only a few months earlier, we were cutting lumps out of each other in an All-Ireland final and here we were standing shoulder to shoulder to mark the sudden passing of Cormac.

A brilliant, courageous act by Armagh.

The whole occasion clearly demonstrated the esteem in which Cormac was held. Cormac was sheer class and so was the send-off that he got.

WHILE THE EXACT cause of Cormac's passing isn't clearly understood, established health experts put his death down to Sudden Adult Death Syndrome. It's a heart condition that often goes undetected in many young people.

Cormac was taken.

I survived my event.

I find it hard to reconcile that at times.

The great Irish GAA commentator, Mícheál Ó Muircheartaigh recited the poem, *The Beautiful Game* at the graveside following his interment.

'All over Ireland they speak of your name…

And the way that you played the beautiful game.'

The line stuck with me. It embedded itself in my head.

I had other lines too. Snippets of that day and various other events and times that we shared with Cormac. I'd a burning desire to do something about them.

I'd go on to compose and record the song *The Brantry Boy*.

Morning has broken, and I hear the news
Phones they are ringing, there's people confused
There's news that in Eglish, near the village of Moy
That the angels have taken the Brantry Boy

My heart it is breaking, as I stand on the shore
For a friend and a leader, we'll see you no more
Close to your home, where the trout feed on fly
On this dull March morning, I ask myself, why?

The lake it is silent, the water is calm
There's no fishing boats, and there is no fisherman
The Brantry is quiet in the heart of Tyrone
For a captain, a hero, a legend has gone

A Gael in his short life, he gave so much joy
Now I bid farewell to the Brantry Boy

Goodbye, God bless as we carry you high

Shoulder to shoulder, as the school children cry
The club's guard of honour, stand proud and erect
As your teammates mourn their gallant full back

Through the green fields of Ireland, you will no longer run
Where you wore the red hand for your County Tyrone
All over Ireland, they speak of your name
And the way that you played the beautiful game

Time has moved onwards, to you now I pray
As I pass by your grave, on this autumn day
I turn to a friend, with tears in his eyes
Like me he still misses the Brantry Boy

Now around Tullygiven, where the Oona runs free
I wander alone, but there's someone with me
A swift-footed spirit, moves on in my mind
To be part of the beauty that he left behind

The lake it is silent, the water is calm
There's no fishing boats, and there is no fisherman
The Brantry is quiet in the heart of Tyrone
For a captain, a hero, a legend has gone

If I could see him today, there's one thing I'd tell him
I miss you dear friend, Cormac McAnallen

PART **7**

New York

Hope is not optimism, which expects things to turn out well, but something rooted in the conviction that there is good worth working for.

(Seamus Heaney)

FROM THE FIRST moment to the last, New York sucks you right in and never gives up.

The very first time I went there, I was 14, on a trip with my grandmother, Maggie to see my uncles, Tony and Francie who were living in Edison, New Jersey.

We were there for six whole weeks.

At that age, I couldn't make much sense of it.

I just remember being consumed by the sense of how quickly everyone moved around the place and the food which was literally available on every single street corner. It just felt a million miles away from where I was raised, but I was hooked.

Totally *hooked.*

The next time I visited, I was 17, shortly after I'd quit school. My mother also had two brothers in Philadelphia, Brian and Thomas Curran.

I arrived shortly before St Patrick's Day and stayed with my uncle, Brian in northeast Philly. He looked after me and got me a few gigs around a few Irish bars in Philadelphia where I got paid to play music.

I became accustomed to that kind of American city lifestyle.

I ended up staying there for around nine months. I loved the place. I loved the life and then there was the extra money that I made playing music. One St

Patrick's Day, I totted up all the cash I made that day by going from bar to bar...
$1,600.

For one day's work.

I remember thinking after that, *I'm going nowhere!* Why would I? By Christmas, I'd be back home in Ireland. Back in Ardboe.

Making money playing a bit of music in the bars was great, but the option to make $1,600 a day relying solely on playing music were days that were very few and far between.

I spent another two years at home, before travelling to New York in 1999; the year I was on the Tyrone football panel under manager, Danny Ball.

That year we had beaten Fermanagh in the opening round of the championship, but in the next game, the hottest day of the summer, we were run into the ground during our warm-up at Killyman GAA pitch. And Down ended up beating us by five points.

I sat on watching the game as an unused substitute.

Waiting.

Patiently waiting.

A COUPLE OF weekends later I was on a plane to New York. That trip gave me a chance to apply for one of the weekend sanctions to play football for one of the teams in New York.

I wasn't the only county player on the plane. The Moortown twins, Chris and Stephen Lawn were also making the journey, as was their clubmate, Brian 'Brew' Quinn. The four of us joined the Tyrone GAA club in New York.

That was my first experience playing in Gaelic Park.

If you were Irish in New York and you'd any interest in the GAA, then Gaelic Park was the place to be. We had a fantastic time there. I can't imagine the number of connections that have been made in and around Gaelic Park over the years that have led to relationships of all sorts, from business through to marriages, and who knows what else.

When the football ended in New York, we returned home to County Tyrone.

The following year, when the new Tyrone manager, Eugene McKenna asked me to go back into the Tyrone senior football panel, I turned it down.

I'd decided that the time had come to travel back to Philadelphia and spend more time there, and I ended up staying for a year.

I was working with my uncle Brian during the day and playing gigs at night wherever I could get them. Looking back, I probably should have taken the offer from Eugene McKenna to join the Tyrone team.

But we are all self-made. We are all a product of our own choices. I am where I am today simply because of the choices that I made.

I returned back to Ardboe shortly before Christmas and after the new year arrived, I put the head down and worked at securing a place on the Ardboe senior team. The club league started in April. We had a decent enough start to the league, but by the end of the first week in May we were out of the club championship and our season was basically over.

Thoughts turned immediately of a return to the United States.

I opted against it.

I hung around home for another few months before taking up an opportunity to spend the summer in Santa Ponsa in Mallorca, Spain.

When I left Holy Trinity College in Cookstown, I had few qualifications to my name. I passed GCSE level Technology, Music and PE. I'd always known deep down that I was much better academically than the performance that I put in while at school.

I'd always wanted to prove that I was better than three GCSE passes.

My decision to do something about it came from a conversation that I had with Mickey Harte at a training session in Edendork, one night in 2003. He mentioned that his wife, Marian was embarking on an Open University course and that it might well be something that I would be interested in pursuing.

That's exactly what I did.

A couple of months later I was enrolled and taking part in a Social Science degree through the Open University. The course was a mixture of lectures in Belfast and reading. Lots and lots of reading. It taught me a lot about managing time.

I picked up a lot, from my teammates, about the mindset required to study. Once, on a bus journey to Cork to play a league game, I was sitting beside Cormac McAnallen. I'd a stack of books on my knee trying to cram in some last-minute revision ahead of an exam the next day.

Cormac was always interested in all types of learning. He ate books. It was no coincidence that he went on to become a teacher. I spent the time on that bus journey bouncing things off him. He was an encyclopaedia of knowledge.

Despite all the encouragement and help, I was finding it difficult to combine work, studying and academic life. The Cork league game was at 2pm on a Sunday. I wasn't back home in Ardboe for another 11 hours.

A 1am bedtime in the early hours of Monday, after a long day away never really helped a 6:30am alarm.

Something would have to give.

Eventually.

*A lot of times I find that people who are blessed with the most talent don't
ever develop that attitude, and the ones that aren't blessed in that way are
the most competitive, and have the biggest heart*

(Tom Brady, American Footballer)

I MANAGED TO juggle study, football, and work for about two years before I
had to let something go.

My degree tutorials were face-to-face and that meant jumping into the car and
travelling down to Belfast, to either Queen's University or Stranmillis University
College.

The tutorial always happened on a Saturday morning and whilst that worked
for me, some people had other ideas. One Saturday morning I was about to jump
into the car when I heard a knock at the front door. It was our senior football
manager in Ardboe.

'Mickey, why aren't you at training?'

I knew that Ardboe had an early Saturday morning training session but I was
under pressure to keep going with my study and something had to give. I hadn't
factored Ardboe training into my thinking at all. I'd told him at the previous
training session that I had other plans, but it obviously didn't register with me.

'I'm getting ready to go to Belfast. I'm going down to university.'

He stood there for a minute... and stared at me.

'You are doing... what?'

He took a few seconds to consider what I just told him, and then he burst out laughing. He couldn't grasp the fact that I was going to a university. How could a drop-out from school with three GCSEs to his name pursue a degree course?

I just wasn't being taken seriously. I'd a choice to make. Stick to my guns and go to Belfast... or go to the training session. I threw the books in the corner, grabbed my gear, and went to training.

It wasn't his fault.

All he did was shine a light on the doubts in my own mind.

My confidence levels were always fluctuating. All that, despite the fact that I'd a letter from the Head of Faculty congratulating me on a score of 96 for one of the modules that I'd completed. I'd got that result over the phone while I was in Dubai with the Tyrone squad. A team holiday as reward for winning the 2003 All Ireland title.

The road to an Open University degree ended over a decision about an Ardboe training session on a Saturday morning.

I NEEDED A change in direction.

That came with a new job in 2004. I joined a company called Composite Design in Omagh. I wasn't a qualified Quantity Surveyor but that's the job that I ended up doing; estimating jobs and project management work.

That work led to another job. I joined Titan Precast, where I worked for a man called Dan McGuinness. Between those two jobs I'd go on to gain almost seven years' experience in the world of construction.

By 2007, the county game was long gone for me.

I was concentrating solely on club games with Ardboe. The season didn't end well for me. We were drawn to play Aghyaran at home in the last game of the league in October. It was a wet miserable evening.

It was about to become even more miserable.

Half-way through the second-half of the game the ball was kicked into our full-back line. One of our defenders, Eugene Devlin, came out to try to win possession alongside the man he was marking, Martin Penrose. The collision between the two players resulted in the ball spilling in my direction.

As the ball spiralled up into the air, I seized the opportunity and jumped up to catch it. It hit my chest with a thud.

I immediately wrapped my arms around it.

And then it happened… I knew something was wrong long before I landed. Badly wrong.

It all happened in slow motion.

First, I landed on my right foot… I normally land on my left.

SNAP!

My teammate, Kieran Devlin immediately put his hands over his head. I could hear him roaring. It didn't take me long to realise that it wasn't good.

The adrenaline in my veins tried to force me back to my feet. As I did, I looked down to see the sole of my foot pointing back up at me. It takes a second or two for you to process something like that, when you first see it.

It's almost like an out of body experience.

Surely that foot doesn't belong to me?

THANKFULLY, THERE WAS a paramedic from Aghyaran in the crowd watching the game. He came to my aid. He administered some gas and air which really helped. I didn't have any pain initially but then after the adrenaline dropped, it was excruciating.

Big Barry McConville and Benny Hurl, the team manager, helped to carry me off the field on a stretcher and both men stayed with me until the ambulance came.

It took the paramedics 40 minutes to reach Ardboe field.

My brother, Ryan accompanied me to Craigavon Hospital Emergency Unit. The doctor there pulled back the curtain in the cubicle and immediately declared that I needed to be transferred to the Royal Victoria Hospital in Belfast for surgery.

By that stage they had administered enough pain relief to make everything very hazy. I slept like a baby for the remainder of that evening.

The next morning, everything was pinned and screwed, but the visit from the surgeon was another sobering experience.

He told me that I had sustained a spiral break of my fibula and tibia bones in my leg. As far as he was concerned, my footballing career was over. In my own head, that didn't really register as a realistic possibility.

The first operation put me in a cast with pins and screws in my leg, and I was in that cast for nine weeks. When I returned to the hospital the medical team discovered that the bones were not healing, so they had to move on a second plan.

Seven days before Christmas Day, I went back under the knife. The second operation involved taking bone marrow out of my hip which was then pasted into the site of the original break.

Slow healing bone breaks are dangerous. They can lead to gangrene. The loss of blood supply which can cause body tissue to die.

I was in a bad place.

My first experience of dealing with a health-related adversity.

I won't pretend to tell you that I was anything other than depressed where I now found myself. Thankfully, one other person spotted that I needed support.

Sean Cavanagh, a player on the Tyrone senior team, contacted me and suggested that I visit the former Meath manager, Seán Boylan at his Healthcare Clinic in Dunboyne, in County Meath.

Seán runs Dunboyne Herbs which is an integrative healthcare clinic rooted in traditional Irish herbal remedies. He oversees a range of healthcare therapies, including reflexology, acupuncture, and Ki-massage. One of Seán's specialities is post-operative care. I was in a place then emotionally and physically where I needed that kind of support.

Seán Boylan doesn't hide his faith, and that faith very much forms a central part of his business. The first thing that you notice when you enter his work premise is a statue dedicated to the Virgin Mary. At that time, I was far from religious, but you couldn't help but feel a great sense of a healing presence in that building.

Some people might see that as some kind of whacky thought process. I used to think that. Not now. The more that I've thought about it, the more convinced I am that everything that we encounter in our lives has some part to play in who we are and how we react to situations that we are presented with.

Seán applied a treatment that involved wrapping my wound in something that looked like a slice of ham. He told me to cut off a piece of it and wrap it in cling film, and place it around my leg every night and sleep with it on. He also gave me a jar of liquid which to me looked like iced tea. He told me to drink a tablespoon of it every day.

Two days before I visited Seán Boylan's office, I went to the Royal Victoria Hospital in Belfast for an x-ray. They told me at the time that my bone was very slow to heal. An X-ray two weeks after my visit to Seán showed that my bone had fully healed.

I couldn't quite believe it.

The day after that second x-ray I got into the car and I drove back to Seán Boylan's office. I wanted to know exactly what had happened me? Seán is also one of the greatest gaelic football managers in the history of the GAA, and he led Meath to four All-Ireland senior titles in the 1980s and 90s. He probably doesn't even remember me or probably doesn't even remember saying this to me, but what he said stuck with me and will forever.

'Mickey, we come from the dirt.

'We return to the dirt.

'All our healing is in the dirt'.

At the time I hadn't the sense to compute what he meant by that. Those words would finally resonate with me much further down the line.

My journey back to full fitness went really well. Within six months, I was back out on the football pitch playing with Ardboe.

By the end of the 2008 season, just over 12 months after I suffered that career threatening leg break, I was Club Player of the Year.

The tunes are belting in the corner
And I, I'm crying in my beer
It's another lonely night in New York City
How I wish to God that you were here

We'll sing our songs until the morning
Of our dreams, our villages and towns
For illegal I am, an undocumented man
Dreaming is all I have for now

Your green rolling hills
Your rivers and your streams
Your mountains and your valleys
I'd walk them in my dreams

This town it makes you tough
There's no time to grieve or pity
The ground will eat you up
Here in New York City

(*Undocumented Man* from Mickey Coleman's *Last Glance* album)

BY 2011 I was content with how life was going.

I had a solid job paying decent enough money. I'd bought a house in Rossa Court, in Ardboe. I was playing football and enjoying it, and some nights I was playing a bit of music in the pubs around home.

I was settled. Or at least I thought I was.

I got a phone call one day from Seamus McNabb in New York asking me to come out to play for a New York team over there during the summer.

Within a few days I was on a plane to JFK along with my cousin, 'Bella' Campbell. The Ardboe club wasn't happy with us, but it was too good an opportunity to miss out on. We travelled on the 4th July.

SEAMUS MCNABB LIFTED us at JFK and we travelled across the city, towards the Throgs Neck Bridge. As we journeyed over the bridge, we could see all of the fireworks going off all over the Bronx. It was a fantastic sight. I couldn't resist…

'Jesus, Seamus this is class. All those fireworks… they must have known that we are coming!'

We stayed at Seamus' house in Yonkers for a few weeks before we got an apartment there. We had a brilliant summer. The craic was good, and we met some brilliant people. One man in particular took me under his wing and made sure that we were well looked after.

Conor Skeffington was from Killeeshil in County Tyrone but he was now based in New York. I'd never met him before that summer. Conor got me a couple of gigs in a bar called Moriarty's on McLean Avenue in Yonkers, owned by a Cavan man, Seamus Smith.

Every Thursday and Sunday was 'Mickey Coleman Night' in Moriarty's.

Seamus was as passionate about gaelic football as any man I'd ever met, and he had a wealth of knowledge when it came to games, players, and the GAA scene in New York. I really enjoyed spending time with him and listening to his stories. Between talking football, playing music, singing songs, and the drink… we had the time of our lives.

It wasn't all fun and games though.

I was nearly killed with work during the day!

There were no hiding places on a construction site when it came to pouring concrete for Seamus McNabb. It was tough work, and you were made to work hard no matter what the weather was like. After a while, I moved across to work for Martin Donnelly who was originally from Dromore in County Tyrone.

That was the biggest learning experience I ever had. Martin was a proper grafter; I spent my time pouring foundations, laying shutters, and carrying rebar.

The worst jobs I ever had were fishing in Lough Neagh and carrying rebar to Martin Donnelly in about 95 degrees heat. Just like Seamus, there was absolutely no hanging around with Martin.

Yes, the work was hard, but all the time I was being sucked in by how brilliant New York was. Martin was involved with a couple of guys at the time, John Shanahan and Joe Devoy, Waterford men and great fellas. After working for them for some time they offered me an opportunity to take on my first job in New York.

One of the jobs they had going on was based down on 77th and York. Their company was tasked with refurbishing an old historic building and part of that work involved installing new windows.

There was a problem with that. The windows had a layer of asbestos caulk around them. Martin saw problems as opportunities to think differently.

'Mickey, why don't you go away and get the license to remove asbestos… and we could give you that job.'

How could I do that? I knew nothing about removing asbestos. I knew nothing about building my work into a firm… and especially not in New York City.

I wasn't about to let him down though. I wanted to prove that I could stand up on my own and deliver for these men. I didn't know it at the time, but that was the spark that lit the flame. A few days later I was at night school learning all about handling asbestos removal.

If I'd have known what was ahead of me, I probably would never have done it. The day I completed the final exam I got a phone call from the bank back home. It wasn't the best of news. They told me that I was in arrears with my mortgage for the house in Ardboe. The money needed to pay it in the bank back home had depleted.

I was sick to the pit of my stomach.

Here I was, out on a limb, reaching for an exam in New York with an uncertain future… and I was essentially bankrupt.

I was in a bad spot.

The flame of hope offered to me by Martin Donnelly and his company was about to be extinguished, unless I moved quickly.

Sometimes life hits you in the head with a brick. Don't lose faith.
You can't connect the dots looking forward; you can only connect them looking backwards.
So, you have to trust that the dots will somehow connect in your future.
You have to trust in something… your gut, destiny, life, karma… whatever.
This approach has never let me down, and it has made all the difference in my life.

(Steve Jobs, Apple)

MY BACK WAS against the wall.

It was almost through the wall and out the other side.

My chest felt tight and constrained. The reality was that the oxygen of hard cash wasn't flowing. I was on my knees.

So much so, that I had to ask Martin Donnelly for a few dollars just to make sure that I covered the rent and kept myself alive in this City. Martin never hesitated.

He reached into the back of his jeep, pulled out a cheque and made it out to me. I was so grateful to him.

A few weeks later, I repaid him in full.

And, somehow, I passed the exam.

I FILED FOR an asbestos removal license and filled in the forms to set up a new company. Martin came back to me and told me that the job had to start soon. I was told that the license would take about six-to-eight weeks to come through.

I couldn't wait.

I needed to start making money… I needed that to happen soon.

The only way to get real money was to get that license and get to work. After a bit of research, I found out that the license was issued from an office in Albany, New York. I needed to get to that office as soon as possible. I couldn't miss out on this job.

I got a lend of a car from Martin's nephew, Paul Donnelly and I made the three-hour trip out to Albany. I went to the Department of Labour building, and I realised when I got there that the public doesn't get access to that building.

I was so desperate.

Somehow, I managed to bullshit my way through security on the front door and into the reception area. I don't remember what I said to them, but it worked. I got in and met the lady who was in charge of processing the license.

I needed a break and I got one. She was of Irish descent and she was minded to do everything that she could to help me out. By the time that I returned to New York, she had the license faxed to Martin Donnelly.

I was in the game.

A day later, I was on the site.

Working inside the building wasn't an issue but it soon became clear that another fairly significant obstacle was in my way.

I needed to be able to access the asbestos on windows outside of the building. That meant setting up a hanging scaffold.

A hanging scaffold is also known as a suspended scaffold. The platform hangs from an overhead support structure, on the roof of a building. In downtown Manhattan, no one sets up a suspended scaffold without a New York City Construction Code License.

Anyone who applies for a rigging foreman's license to hang a suspended scaffold must have served their time operating one. Step one is therefore a basic operator's license first.

After several years you can apply for a rigging foreman's license. The rigging foreman sets up the scaffold, ties off all the bowlines and safety harnesses, and commissions it ready for use.

Here I was.

Without an operating licence attempting to get a rigging foreman's license.

When I rocked up to the first training session at night school in Queens, the lady taking the course asked me for my operator's license. I told her that I didn't have one. I was never on a suspended scaffold in my life. I couldn't tell her what it looked like.

'You can't take this class.

'You don't have your 30-hour operator's license.'

I told her that I would take it anyway and see how I got on. She told me that there wasn't a chance of me passing it… it was a waste of my time.

I asked her if I could take the course anyway? She told me that it was my $800 and that it was up to me. I sat in the middle of the class with a bunch of experienced suspended scaffold operators all around me, and I listened hard. Very hard.

We were shown a bunch of knots and tie-offs that these men were looking at on a daily basis. The instructor had quite a bit of fun with me throughout the course. She knew all of it was new to me, and she played on that.

I knew that I needed to work twice as hard as the other guys in that class if I was going to get up to speed. No one in there needed this more than I did. YouTube saved my backside. After the opening night, I went home, and I sat there watching YouTube videos on creating knots for suspended scaffolds.

I needed something to practice on. I reached into the wardrobe and pulled out two neck ties and I spent my evenings using YouTube to practice tying bowlines.

YouTube and two neck ties.

What the f**k was I doing with two neck ties in Yonkers, New York?

I spent night after night tying every bowline that you could name, and every other knot needed to build that scaffold.

Part of the final exam was a practical. They gave you a rope scaffold flat on the ground and you had to build it. It required expertise in tying off four different knots. I went into the exam and practical, and aced both of them. Two men jumped into the scaffold that I'd built in the practical and they had to hoist it.

It worked perfectly.

I'd done it. I'd beaten the odds.

Instead of me paying out $2,000 a week for a rigging foreman, I was now the rigging foreman. I remember the first day that I got onto my own scaffold at a site.

I wouldn't put anyone else on it until I got onto it myself.

PULSE

THE FIRST MAN to get onto the scaffold with me was an Ecuadorian, called William Negriti. I'd set up a 'C hook' off the wall on the roof and was about to see if we could hoist my first suspended scaffold using the two motors at either end of it.

I was sick with pressure.

My heart was pounding in my chest.

William was on one of the motors and I was operating the other one... at the opposite side of the scaffold. 'Take her up a foot, William!'

It worked.

'Let's try and take it up one storey.'

Everything felt stable... apart from my nerves.

Before we knew it, we were at the top... and I was on top of the world.

Every couple of days, I'd move the rig for the next set of windows. That 22-foot scaffold moving slowly along those columns of windows... one day at a time. Then around the corner... and on to the next set of windows.

Conor Skiffington would come down on a Saturday and help me to move the rig and motors around to the next side of the building. It meant that on a Monday morning, the men were able to come in and begin their run.

IT WAS 2012.

My company Shoreline Builders consisted of three people.

William Negreti.

His son, William.

And me.

I was up and running.

THAT WAS THE first time in my life that anyone outside of my own family had put a bit of faith in me to succeed in running a business. Martin Donnelly saw something in me, and he backed it.

That was the kick-start for me.

Without a question, Martin Donnelly gave me an opportunity in life that transformed it forever.

I'll never forget that, or what he did for me.

I travelled back to Ireland to spend Christmas at home but I knew that things had changed for me. My future was in New York.

My work was in New York.

My new business was in New York.

A business that I owned.

THAT TIME At home gave me a chance to apply for my visa, and by then I'd rented my house out in Ardboe.

Everything was back on track with my mortgage repayments and the general bills that come with running a property were being paid. Whilst I had moved out of that house, some of my clothes were still in bags in the garage.

I went through all of my Tyrone gear and stumbled upon the Tyrone jersey that was signed by Cormac McAnallen and all of the players on the 2003 panel.

By some stretch, that was my most precious possession.

I was so relieved to find it.

I knew immediately who I was giving it to.

I placed it into the suitcase and flew back to New York after Christmas and went to visit Martin Donnelly.

I wanted to thank him for what he had done for me. *What could I offer the man?* He didn't need my money.

All that I could do was give him something that meant *everything* to me.

It took a lot of persuasion from me for him to accept it.

Thankfully, he did.

ONE JOB LED to another and, all the time, I was adding to and chopping the number of staff I was employing. One week it might be three.

The next week five.

The next week 10 and then… maybe back to three again.

My first purchase was a white van that doubled up as a work and gig machine. It kept breaking down on me. I rented a little garage under my apartment for $150 a week off Dermot and Trina Flemming in Yonkers.

Shoreline had its first base. My business grew, and with it the contacts that I'd established in New York. The Irish network in the construction industry in New York is well established and one of the first things that Irish company owners want to know is… where are you from?

When I told them that I was from County Tyrone, that would normally follow with a second question.

'You must know Fay Devlin then?' I'd no idea who Fay Devlin was; the only Fay Devlin that I knew was the man that played corner-back for Tyrone and my fellow teammate on the Ardboe team that won the championship.

I knew for certain that he wasn't based in New York.

By 2012, I'd heard this Fay Devlin man's name 100 times, but I'd never met him. His name kept coming up with such frequency that I felt I needed to meet him. By then, I knew that he was behind a very successful construction company called Eurotech.

I was told that he had a serious interest in gaelic football and Irish music. I only found out later that he was hearing similar things about me.

'You must know Mickey Coleman?'

'Mickey is out here and he has set up his own company.'

We were moving in similar circles but our paths had never crossed. One of my jobs put me in contact with Paul O'Brien, who ran a company called Pinnacle Environmental. Every year the Friends of Sinn Fein have a big networking event in New York, and on one occasion Paul invited me along to be a guest at his table.

All the kingpins of New York construction were at that gig.

Before the dinner in New York people usually met up in Rosie O'Grady's Bar across the street from the hosting hotel. It was there that I finally met Fay. It was a fabulous first meeting and we shared plenty of craic over the fact that this first meeting had taken some time to come to pass.

At the time, I didn't know it, but that was the start of something big for me. Fay would go on to become my closest ally in navigating the world of New York construction.

Today he is my mentor and one of my closest friends.

PART 8

Erin

IT WAS 2013.

I'd only been in the United States for less than one year when I was asked if I would come in and coach the New York senior football team.

Connie Molloy had only just been appointed manager of the team by the New York County Board. His brother was the legendary, Anthony, who captained Donegal to the 1992 All-Ireland title, made famous by his speech at the end of game when he collected the trophy.

'Sam's for The Hills!'

Connie and I hit it off immediately.

He was my kind of guy. He was boisterous, but kind and full of energy. He didn't give a damn what people thought of him. Conny's son, CJ was on the team.

That connection with New York GAA offered me a few new work connections.

That's the GAA the world over.

Our backroom team consisted of Tony McTigue from Mayo and Davy Byrne from Longford. We had a great connection, and we had some great nights talking through tactics and such matters. All enhanced by the sinking of a few pints on McLean Avenue.

We were really confident in our ability to do a good job.

I'd never coached a senior side before. The extent of my coaching knowledge had been limited to helping train underage teams in Ardboe.

That didn't stop me and I was excited to be involved. It didn't take long to work out that it was an unglamorous job. Training for the New York team at that time took place mainly in the winter months. Quite often the weather was anything but helpful.

It was really poor.

At that point I lived in an apartment off McLean Avenue in Yonkers.

One of those freezing cold and wet nights in February I'd just finished a coaching session in Gaelic Park. Before I went home, I stopped off in a little place close to the apartment called Eileen's Kitchen. The decision to stop there would spark off a chain of events that would bring someone very special into my life.

While we were grabbing something to eat, Joanie Madden from Cherish the Ladies, Aidan's band, came across and sat down beside us for a chat. I'd known Joanie for some time before that; she was one of the first people I'd met from the music scene when I first came out to New York in early 2012. Back then I relied on her for a PA system that I needed for some of the gigs that I'd do in various pubs across New York.

It wasn't long before Joanie got talking about a cruise that she runs, aptly named the 'Folk n Irish Cruise'.

TRY SAYING THAT one with a few beverages in you.

Every year the cruise ship would go out of harbour in Miami and travel around a number of the popular resort islands of the Caribbean. She explained that she was getting ready to fly down to Florida.

'Actually Mickey, one of the musicians, Eddi Reader is not able to come on the cruise this time around as her husband is unwell. Could you fill in for her?'

My head was in a whirl. I'd only started Shoreline at the time. I told her that I'd need to scramble a few men around and see what was possible. I asked her if she could wait a few days for an answer? Joanie Madden isn't a lady who hangs around.

She needed an answer there and then.

I gave in. I told her I'd go.

I had no idea how I would make this happen, but I was buzzing all the same about the thought of travelling around the Caribbean playing Irish music on a cruise ship.

What could be better?

When I got back to the apartment, I made a few phone calls and got work covered for the following week. Two days later, I grabbed my guitar and a small bag and jumped into a mini-van with Joanie and a bunch of other musicians. I was on my way to LaGuardia Airport to catch a flight to Miami.

I knew a couple of the guys in the van already. Padraig Allen was on board, a nephew of Tony Allen from the Irish band, Foster and Allen. John Nolan, the box player, was also in the van. A few hours later, I was standing in Miami about to board the ship which would be our home for a week.

The Joannie Madden Cruise is extremely popular with Irish Americans and is based on a Norwegian cruise-liner out of Miami. The route takes in St Thomas and Tortola in the Virgin Islands, and on to Nassau in the Bahamas. It always featured a string of popular Irish musicians, such as Mary and Frances Black, Sharon Shannon, Lúnasa, Susan McCann, and Tommy Sands.

As we waited there, a taxi pulled up alongside us and out jumped two young ladies, a young man, and an older man. They immediately made their way over to Padraig and he was greeted with hugs and kisses.

'This is Mickey.'

Padraig introduced me to one of the ladies… Erin.

I was immediately drawn to her eyes and her smile. I was then introduced to Erin's sister, Nadine, her brother, John-Paul and her stepfather, John. As we were about to board the ship, I noticed that Erin had a violin case on her back with a number of stickers on it.

There it was in front of me.

A County Tyrone crest on a sticker right beside a County Kerry crest sticker.

After all the battles that we had while playing with Tyrone against Kerry in the leagues and championships, and here in Miami was a very pretty girl uniting the two counties on a violin case.

I was hooked.

I couldn't resist.

AFTER I BOARDED, I was allocated my room and left my luggage there to go exploring. Your first time on a ship of that size is a serious experience.

It was huge!

A city on the high seas, as I was to find out.

I made my way up onto the top deck where somebody allocated me a card that would provide me with free drink for the week. What a dangerous little piece of plastic that was!

It was there that I met Erin for the second time. I took my opportunity.

'What's with the Tyrone and Kerry stickers on the violin case?'

She told me that her father, Frankie Loughran was from Tyrone and her mother, Marjorie was from Kerry. That was my chance to play up my Tyrone-ness, to which she replied that Frankie was originally from Pomeroy.

Pomeroy's claim to fame is that it is the highest village in the North of Ireland. It's only thirty 30 minutes from where I was raised in Ardboe. This was uncanny.

It was mainly only small talk after that, but later that evening we ended up playing a music session together in one of the bars on the ship, alongside John Nolan. I was absolutely blown away by how talented she was with the violin. I recall asking John about her after one of the numbers and he told me that she was very well known in Irish music circles in New York. I felt that I must have been living under a stone not to have come across her before.

The next day, we gathered for Mass on the ship in one of the dining rooms.

Like many a good Irishman, Mass provided a perfect opportunity to settle the head and view the options life presented you with.

I recall being not as focused on the ceremony that day as I should have been.

Erin was most definitely in my mind and within my eyesight. This was one very attractive lady. I accidently on purpose got chatting with her once again after Mass.

On the third night, we got to spend time with two very famous Irish musicians, Sharon Shannon and Mary Black. The conversations with Erin got a little more intense that evening. I've been asked since did it not occur to me that Erin's stepfather, John was knocking about in the background.

It didn't seem to phase me.

Perhaps it was that little bit of plastic I'd been allocated and the drink that gave me the courage, but I've a feeling it really wouldn't have mattered. It was nothing too serious with Erin during that week, but we had a fantastic time on the cruise, and everyone really enjoyed themselves. All light-hearted in nature. I met a lot of amazing people, many of whom I still regard as good friends right up to this day.

Erin and I obviously realised that we lived only a few minutes away from each other in Woodlawn. A few days after we got back, I got a phone call from her, and she asked me to meet her in The Heritage Bar on McLean Avenue, alongside some of the people who had been on the cruise.

It was really after that evening that we decided we would become a little more serious about each other. All of that was reinforced by our mutual love of traditional Irish music. It made sense for us to meet up and play Irish sessions together in a range of bars throughout New York.

It was the perfect excuse just to hang out together.

I've been in a number of relationships and it's very difficult for someone who isn't a musician to understand what it means to perform music for an audience. Inevitably, that involves being on the road several nights in the month. There's a real, life-affirming power when playing music and a pull towards it when you are away from it.

Erin and I were very much on common ground with our music. It was so easy for both of us.

When we became close it was such an important part of both of our lives and it still is. Erin introduced me to a wide range of Irish American musicians. My circle of friends in New York widened and that in turn brought links with many people that I'd go on to do business with.

Up to then, I'd been sticking to the Irish people that I'd known. Through Erin,

I was like a seed full of great ideas and now I was beginning to grow into Irish American society.

They say that when you've met the right person, you'll quickly understand that that's the person you want to spend your life with. I knew that early on with Erin. I'd met her in February 2013, and by the late summer we were both on a flight back to Ireland to see Tyrone take on Mayo in an All-Ireland semi-final.

Ireland was familiar territory for Erin.

She'd studied for five years in the University of Limerick and she had visited her relatives in Pomeroy numerous times. She knew a lot of the same people that I'd known when I was growing up in Tyrone. I'd known her uncles and her cousins, because I'd gone to post primary school with some of them.

It took a cruise ship in Miami to piece us together.

PULSE

THE FOLLOWING FALL, I recorded an album with Gabriel Donoghue in Philadelphia; a seriously talented musician. We decided that we would launch the album on the Joannie Madden cruise in February, a year on from my first experience of the trip.

A few days prior to launch I made my way down to the 'Diamond District' in New York City and purchased an engagement ring.

The night we launched the album Last Glance, I proposed to Erin. The proposal happened at the end of one of the songs, after I had called her up onto the stage to accompany me.

Deep breaths as she walked up to the stage.

It was time.

I looked around me, quickly, at the audience.

People we knew, some we didn't.

I looked at Erin.

I dropped to one knee.

It was... time.

Breathe...

And I got the words out, amazingly, in the right order... I think!

Thankfully, I got the response that I was looking for.

WE GOT MARRIED in New York a month later, but we wanted to have an Irish wedding so that was planned in for August of that same year. The wedding took place in the Church of the Assumption in Moyvane in County Kerry in August 2014, the homeplace of Erin's grandmother, with our wedding reception in the Listowel Arms.

The wedding was on a Thursday and on Friday we went out to the Cliff House Hotel in Ballybunion, where a music session was organised to celebrate our marriage. It was attended by several hundred of our wider family circles and a number of the Tyrone senior squad with whom I'd played with between 2003 and '05.

Most of the lads who travelled stayed for a couple of days and then returned home. One member of the team, namely Owen 'Mugsy' Mulligan, decided to stay a while longer. Himself and a member of An Garda Siochana had a conversation that delayed Owen's return to the North. Owen claims that the Garda was a big fan of his and that he'd only stopped him for an autograph. He must have been a really big fan of Owen's because the word is that he offered Owen free accommodation.

Mugsy used his charm to meet all the requests and is still treated as an absolute legend in Kerry to this day.

Erin and I set up home in Woodlawn, New York.

We rented a two-bedroom apartment and then bought our own house in Woodlawn after our first son Micháel arrived in January 2015.

When Erin returned to New York after college she set up her own school of music. The Loughran School of Music is based out of the Music House in Woodlawn and is now one of the most prestigious Irish Traditional Music

Schools in North America. She worked there most evenings. It was full-on.

She is incredible with kids. I think she was born to teach music to children. There are now dozens of children from her school who have won New York and All-Ireland Fleadh medals within their music instrument discipline. She loves her work and I know that those kids love her. What an incredible thing to be able to pass on a passion for music.

Our son, Riordan, arrived in 2018, the day before Tyrone played in the All-Ireland final against Dublin. There had been more than a fleeting thought in my mind that I could catch a flight to Dublin for the game, but I knew better than to even mention it. Erin is a very understanding woman but there is a limit to that understanding, and that wasn't the weekend to stretch it.

In November 2019, Riordan developed a fever at home.

We took him immediately to the nearest hospital, but we were sent home a few hours later after they told us that he would be fine. The next morning, I woke up and got the train into New York for work. It was still dark when I got off the train, when I got a phone call from Erin. She was concerned about a rash that had broken out on Riordan.

Erin rang the paediatrician and took him immediately to the Emergency Room at Westchester Medical Centre. I left a meeting with Patsy Donnelly and Fay Devlin, and rushed to Westchester. I was met in the door by a doctor, who explained that Riordan had developed some type of infectious disease and that they needed to work quickly. The plan was to run a blood transfusion immediately.

We spent two weeks in that Medical Centre as Riordan fought for his life. He was incredibly sick. They never really were able to get to the bottom of what it was.

They thought it might be Stevens-Johnson syndrome; a rare but serious disorder of the skin and muscle membranes. Thankfully, the top layer of the infected skin died and started to shed as the days progressed. That was a tough few weeks.

He recovered well and got back to full health.

AT THAT TIME, Erin was working with Shoreline in the mornings and then running her own school of music in the evenings. She was working 12- to 13-hour days. There was a point that I clearly recall where we looked at each other in the hospital room, and asked ourselves what exactly we were doing?

There was a realisation that our kids were growing up and we weren't around to see enough of them. We never saw our children; all we did was work.

Things completely changed from that point forward. Erin's time at Shoreline had to come to an end. She was going to spend more time at home with the kids and work in her school of music in the evenings.

Every interest that I had, Erin seemed to share it with me. For a long time, people didn't take me seriously when I spoke to them about my ambitions of setting up a successful business in New York and having an office in Manhattan.

Many of those people laughed at me.

Perhaps they'd known me from home and thought that guy will amount to nothing other than someone who's up for a bit of craic and a few pints. They didn't see that I had the ability to do well. Erin always saw that in me.

No matter how silly my dreams and aspirations, she would support them.

She never once laughed at me or said that you are dreaming. Her mantra has always been the same.

'Go for it. Go for it, Mickey!'

She never once questioned it; she has always had so much belief in me. That's a massive driving force for me. Erin's belief in me is such a core part of where I am today.

Erin is a private person but she's confident in her thoughts and outlook on life. No matter what issue we were faced with, I always really focused in on what she was saying. She's always had my best interest at heart and she's very astute with her advice.

When you hear the words, 'Mickey, you might want to think about that again.' you know that you are most likely on the wrong track. We work well together, and we bounce off each other in a really positive way.

We weren't the kind of couple that, prior to my heart attack, were overly demonstrative in terms of a kiss or a hug in public. That has changed. I couldn't care less who sees us now. You never know when you will have lived your last moment, so live a little.

All moments are special.

PART **9**

Total Faith

AS I'VE EXPLAINED before, there's a loneliness associated with serious illness.

The reality of illness nails you firmly into that space.

Perspective leaves you.

You are flushed clean of perspective. It's all about you and the negative thoughts that wash over you and consume your mindset.

Truth is, the impact of illness is shared far beyond your own selfish single-minded view of the world.

There were so many people that were impacted by my widow-maker heart attack that I will never be able to properly acknowledge all of them.

Erin was thrown into something neither of us had been prepared for. She dropped everything to be there for me in that hospital. Her support, care and attention continue to inspire me. She has been incredible.

My two boys, Micháel and Riordan! Yes, the novelty of Granny Margie looking after both of them might well have been great at the start but I've no doubt they were impacted by myself and Erin not being around. Despite that, Margie got them ready for school every morning and they never missed a day. The story of us being on vacation for a few days will linger in their mind for some time.

Not sure how Erin managed to convince them, when she told them that she was home to shower because she didn't like the shower in the hotel where we were staying.

My brother, Raymond, who jumped into the car that night and drove for over two hours to support Erin in the hospital. Erin's sister, Ned who cleared everything that she might have previously committed to in order to support Erin.

My parents, and my brothers and sisters.

When someone takes ill at home, most relatives are only minutes if not less than an hour or so away from them. Not so in my case. I was over 3,000 miles away and getting across to New York from Ardboe isn't the most straightforward trip to negotiate. How must my mother, Teresa and my sister, Andrea have felt leaving Ardboe, driving to Dublin and flying to New York? How must they have hoped that I'd live to see them arrive at the hospital.

Maureen and Gerald Conroy, my neighbours from across the street, looked after our two kids until Erin's mother got to our house, and she basically lived there until we returned home.

Nurse Monica at Montefoire Hospital, who was due to go home after her shift, but decided to stay on to support Erin while I was going through the operation to insert the stent.

The ICU doctor, Dr Kavak, who told Erin that he couldn't sleep the night after they took me off the ventilator because he was so worried about me. He sat outside my room the whole of the next day monitoring my vitals and being there to reassure Erin. There were nurses coming to him about other patients' downstairs, but he told them that he needed to be there as I was the sickest person in the hospital right at that time. Dr Kavak was probably more worried about me, than either I or Erin will ever know.

Rory Healy, a Clarkstown police sergeant, and his wife, Melissa, who are two of our closest friends in Pearl River. They went over and above their daily routine to support Erin and our family members during my hospital stay.

Derek Barry my operations manager, and all the staff at Shoreline. Derek not only visited the hospital but kept the show on the road with the business during what must have been a challenging time for everyone in the office.

My Tyrone GAA colleagues on the 2003 All Ireland winning team and backroom team. They sent those messages of best wishes at a time when they weren't all that sure if I'd ever recover enough to view them.

The many hundreds and thousands of people, some of whom I know, many of whom I don't, who took time out to send me a message on social media, via email and good old-fashioned mail.

YOU THINK YOU are alone.

You are convinced you are alone.

You are alone.

But the impact of your illness spreads out much wider than your broken and deflated ego.

It's like throwing a stone into a lake. You might not always see or hear it, but the impact of that stone on the water has a much more profound resonance on the environment around it than you might believe.

My widow-maker set a chain of events in place, that I'd no control over.

In the days, weeks and months since that event, I've been contacted by a large number of people that I know who have gone for the dye test. Many of them discovered that they are on the wrong side of the curve and have been advised to change their lifestyle, and start some medication.

Never underestimate the impact of your illness on others.

Sometimes the ripples of impact extend much wider than you think.

No ifs.
No buts.
No maybes.
Total faith.

(Tyrone Senior Footballers, 2003)

HAVE I CHANGED?

I don't look too far ahead these days to be honest.

Today is today, and believe me I'm very grateful for it. There's a great sense of gratitude that I have now, that I didn't have before. I know that for people looking in on my story, there's a great recovery to be noted.

But I've never really shook off the cloud above my head. I still need to be careful. I need to be sensible in how I look after myself. The odd time I take a pain in the back or the arm… or the leg, and Ill be thinking… *Oh shit! What's this?*

Small and silly things stop me in my tracks sometimes and make me refocus. Take life insurance; most insurance companies will never look at me again. I'm a liability that they are not prepared to take a risk on anymore.

Eventually I got on the phone to a broker, and they agreed to get me onto a deal. I now pay quadruple the money any normal healthy guy would pay to cover the plan. The current plan is for five years. That gets you thinking about whether or not I'll get through the next five years.

Every day I'll think, right I need to get to the gym.

I need to strengthen my heart.

There's still work to me done there.

I'm still ambitious.

That 'day' has given me more drive than I've ever had before.

The things that I used to be fragile about have long disappeared. Making that call for a sale. Going to meet a potential customer that I'd never met before and worrying about it. Giving my opinion. It never happens now.

I'd rock up onto Pennsylvania Avenue and meet the President in the White House now. It wouldn't cost me a thought.

It's not important. It's really not important anymore.

I say to myself all the time, 'Mickey, if you think you are having a bad day, take a walk up through a hospital ward… and think again'.

I'd a business meeting with a general contractor a few months back and he was fretting about the fact that my guys weren't off the site in time to meet his schedule. There were changes to the job and we needed extra time to get everything cleared up. He was really exercised about it and stressed out. He probably didn't sleep all that well after he spoke to me.

I slept like a baby. If that guy got out of bed tomorrow morning and had pains in his chest, the very last thing that he would be thinking about is getting a job finished.

I'm very fortunate.

I got the kick in the backside and recovered to understand that.

The vast majority of people will never get that kick in the backside, and they will never understand it. I'd love to be able to bottle the feeling and hand it to them.

In the grand scheme of life, the jobs will always get done.

Someone will step up and get them over the line.

You'll not always have your health.

It's just not worth the hassle.

Yes, I'll plan.

I'll plan for down the line, but I don't take it for granted.

ERIN WILL TELL people that I'm much more lenient with the kids these days than I was before. Every single thing that they do doesn't bother me anymore. I used to be a little bit more irritable from time to time. I won't let them run riot and I can be firm with them when I need to be.

I'm reluctant to go into overdrive on this but I'm more open to the spiritual side of life. *How could I not be?* I've been to the edge of life.

I'm also a lot more positive than I was before. Those who knew me before the heart attack will tell you that I normally had a positive spin on things, but that perhaps has a little more depth to it these days, because I believe in it.

I just don't sweat on the same things the way that I used to do in the past.

What I do now, more so than in the past, is set out my plans to achieve something and I get fully invested in it. My rehab had loads and loads of milestones that I openly shared with Erin and the rehab team in Montefoire Nyack. When I set goals, I get obsessed with them. When you get obsessed with achieving something, it's surprising how many times that you do.

I view people through a new lens these days.

WHEN I GO into work meetings with guys who appear to be disgruntled and angry about something, I just think they aren't at peace with themselves. I don't try to change them.

I try to be the person that I want others to be.

I ask myself the question, would I want to hang around with someone who is behaving the way that I am behaving? It's a great way to find balance in your temperament. It's amazing how many times that a friendly hello can open up a conversation that gets you and the person that you are talking with into a positive mindset.

I've found a way to be receptive and positive to whatever position that I find myself in. The former Tyrone GAA senior football manager, Mickey Harte often said that we normally find ourselves in places that we don't want to be. The players that respond best to handling those types of places are the players who are prepared to be in them, and who accept it and do something to get out of it.

Get creative, look out for opportunities, and hang out with the people that approach everything with a can-do attitude.

I'M VERY THANKFUL.

My business continues to grow. I'm still learning. I'm still very hands on, and I suppose that needs to change if I'm going to build up some capacity. I still like the buzz of running it. The plan is to make the business run itself, someday… but I enjoy and love what I'm doing too much to make that day anytime soon.

I love driving down into the city.

Meeting up with people like Fay Devlin and some of the other business owners that have helped me get onto my feet. I'm not doing it eight hours a day, every day, like I used to.

Again, gaelic football taught me a lot about achieving success. See it, be it.

Tyrone had never won a senior All-Ireland title back at the beginning of 2003, but that never stopped our group of players acting like we hadn't. We had it engrained into our psyche that we were All Ireland champions long before we landed the Sam Maguire trophy.

Every day that team took to the field, they acted as if they were going for their second or third All Ireland crown. There was an arrogance.

An entitlement.

A belief.

A belief summarised in the mantra that became a theme for that panel.

"No ifs.

'No buts.

'No maybes.

'Total faith.'

YONKERS IS A city in itself, situated in Westchester County, to the north east of Manhattan. It was, and still is, the 'go to' district for anyone from Ireland hoping to get a foothold into New York and the United States.

When Erin and I got married, we bought a house on Woodlawn Avenue in Yonkers and set up our first home there. Like hundreds of other Irish immigrants, Yonkers provided a comfortable and welcoming place for any young twenty-something year old couple to fit right in.

We were surrounded by an Irish community there.

Walk a few yards down MacLean Avenue and you'd be immersed in all aspects of Irish life. Erin and I played music in the bars there quite regularly and there was a real feeling of it being a 'home' away from home. It felt like a big urban Irish parish with all the trappings that brings. It had that kind of a vibe.

Even though we were very content and well settled in Yonkers, it was never going to be our final destination.

Once the two boys came along, we knew that we would like to explore the possibility of finding a place with a little more room. Erin grew up in Pearl River and we had always talked about the possibility of moving up there one day. It made sense to us. It may only have been 40 minutes away from where we lived in Woodlawn Avenue, but we would be closer to Erin's mother and sisters, who still lived up there, and they would be closer to our two boys.

That ticked one of our boxes.

Another small, but important network of people that could support us when we needed them. At that time, we just didn't realise how much we would rely on them.

The second one was easily chalked off, as just like Yonkers, there is a big Irish community in Pearl River. We've always wanted to live in a place that's close to our own Irish culture, and a place that supports and celebrates that culture.

We started looking at houses up there in the fall of 2018 and we spent a lot of time trying to find the right one. Eventually, we found the one we really wanted in the spring of 2019. We agreed the asking price and the property was signed over to us on July 12, 2019. The signing fell on the same date as my cousin, Bella Campbell's, wedding. That annoyed me as he was the guy that I'd first visited America with. There wasn't much that I could so.

In this part of the world, you need to be there in person to sign up on the day. He had to settle for a video message of me wishing him all the best for his big day.

We made the move from Yonkers up to Pearl River a few days later and started to make the normal renovations, tweaks and changes to décor and all that goes with changing a property to make it your own home. The move wasn't really a big deal for me.

I WAS AN immigrant in the United States and it never really mattered to me where I lived. I'd been of that frame of mind since I first stepped foot off the plane. I wanted to live in the United States.

Where I dropped anchor didn't concern me.

Erin and I both knew that we wanted the two boys to get a good education, and Pearl River offered that opportunity. We had good options there. Funny how the priorities change. Funny now, how education became a little more important to me when I was making decisions for my own two sons.

I'll be keeping a closer eye to how they are progressing with their schoolwork than I ever did with my own.

Pearl River offered my family space. We have a big yard. A bigger house than the one we just left. A bit more freedom. It is much quieter. A lot more relaxed.

There aren't as many vehicles on the road.

It's funny how accustomed you become to the hustle and bustle of city life. The city beats with a different pulse. The sights, the smell, and the noise.

Always the noise. The ongoing noise.

Car, van and truck horns everywhere. The drivers around New York can't turn the steering wheel without giving the horn a blast. I'm now one of them. It was nice being able to drive away from the that kind of environment every evening. The opportunity to transition out of the noise and chaos that New York city brings to your daily routine.

The chance to sit out on the back deck, beside the pool and realise that one thing that many people take for granted.

I could hear the birds singing again.

We could walk the two boys to school if we wanted. Wander down into the town at night and get a meal in a local restaurant. Call into one of the Irish bars, and join in on a music session. The lifestyle was different.

Upon reflection, it was maybe too good.

DESPITE THE CHANGE of homes, my workload continued to increase. I'd lost the balance. *Did I really ever have it in the first place?*

My eating habits were poor.

Breakfast normally consisted of something in paper, bought through one of the numerous drive-in establishments on the way into Yonkers. Lunch, if I got it at all, might well have been another fast-food convenience option. On the rare occasion, a slap-up lunch in a downtown or Yonkers restaurant.

The evening option back in the house might well have been my only opportunity to eat a healthy meal throughout the day.

Something had to give.

I was a walking timebomb.

Many of us are.

In the world of work, my business Shoreline Builders Inc, was really taking off. I had a number of jobs secured and in the pipeline. In a place like Manhattan the work never stops. Work for me meant overseeing a series of jobs across multiple sites. All at the same time.

I'd moved home to Pearl River.

Shoreline was still based and operating out of Yonkers.

The reality was that, by the end of 2019, I'd an important decision to make about the location of Shoreline Builders Inc as well.

Most cities are nouns. New York's a verb.

(John F Kennedy)

THERE'S A HALF-TRUTH, or a slight myth in a song that talks about if you can make it here, in New York... you will make it anywhere!

According to a very successful business man and very good friend of mine, 'Building a business in New York is like playing Russian Roulette with a machine gun'.

I can tell you now that if you think you've made it in New York then all that you are is one bad decision away from *never making* it there. It's a big old bear and there's a lot going on in there in the world of business to ever get your head around it all.

Shoreline Builders Inc had a lot of work on and all of it was based in Manhattan. Truth was, our base in Yonkers was in the wrong place. You'd think that having an office in downtown Manhattan would be a crazy place to attempt to save money, but that facts were different.

I'd been weighing the whole thing up for a while. In 2020 the decision was made. A base in Yonkers serving work in Manhattan was costing us more money than establishing an office in the city.

When my team were all based up in the Yonkers office, they all needed Shoreline vehicles to go to and from the jobs across the city. Yonkers didn't offer too many wonderful public transport options.

That meant running a small fleet of vehicles and supporting all the finances that is associated with that... toll-booths, insurance, gas, parking charges, maintenance. It all takes money. That money eats into the margins and without noticing it things can get tight.

It made sense then, to stand up a small office in the city. That meant my team could make their way into the city on public transport and bounce around the various jobs that we had on.

In our game, the construction industry, the biggest cost factor of them all is time.

Time, is one of the key commodities that dictates a successful business from one that's struggling. My guys found that they could visit four or five jobs in the one day and be back in the office in between times to complete change orders and paperwork.

Before, they'd have been lucky to get to a couple of sites in the one day. It wasn't long before the cost of renting the Manhattan office made far more sense than running a fleet of vehicles. It made *complete* sense.

Within a couple of months, I'd brought the number of vehicles down by two thirds.

I decided that the primary business model needed to change as well. Removing asbestos, whilst it paid very well, cost a lot of money to service. We used a lot of heavy equipment, and that equipment needed transportation.

Shoreline Environmental would become Shoreline Builders Inc.

We moved towards installing drywall.

Every floor of every building in New York City has drywall.

Becoming familiar with the planning, installation and construction of that product gave us new energy and if we kept our heads, longevity in a city that doesn't stop building. While there are pockets of brand-new buildings going on all the time around the place, most of the work comes from the clean-out of existing buildings. They are stripped right back to the brick work, and a company like ours goes in and fits them back out.

It might be an old factory space being turned into a modern residential block. It might be an old residential space being repurposed for office space. I read somewhere recently that there are over 47,000 buildings in New York, and an average of 16 floors across those buildings.

With numbers like that, the potential for work in this city never stops.

All that we need is a drywall fitout for half, or even better, one of those floor spaces and we are up and running with a job.

That said, drywalling in NYC is a cut-throat and competitive business. Running a business like this can be done in two ways. You can hire in the guys to do the job and hide away in the background, or you can stand up and be front and centre of the job you've taken on.

I've always been of the opinion though that Shoreline Builders Inc is sold on what I bring to the table. It's my business...

And the buck always stops, with me.

MY WORD IS important.

To some people, that means nothing. To some others, it does.

I'm a firm believer that if you do the right thing by people, that things will always work out in your favour. What are you going to gain by screwing someone for a extra few dollars? What's the point in cutting corners?

I try to be straight up and honest.

'Give Respect, Get Respect'.

It's a logo on the gaelic football referees' jerseys these days. It's only a recent addition. It wasn't there when I was playing, just in case you are talking to some of the men that officiated in some of my games. That's my excuse and I'm sticking to it.

In business you can meet all the crooks you want to meet. You can get yourself easily entwined with all the idiots that you would care to meet. The bottom line for me is that, you sit across the table and have lunch with a person, and you tell him or her that you are going to do something for them... and you deliver.

That person will come back to you with more work, again and again. Regardless of whether you are the most expensive or not. We might well be the most expensive company for some jobs, but if we deliver what we say we are going to deliver, then that normally wins us the contract.

I thrive on winning the trust of people.

I always have. Back when I was playing football my manager would entrust me to do a job, to deliver for the team. Business is exactly the same.

It gives me a similar buzz of energy.

We like to think we do a better job than most of the other companies but the chances are we don't fit drywall better than a range of other competitors, but what gets us to the table is the respect we have for people, and the trust they place in us.

I can talk the talk all day long.

I sell the business every single day.

Talk is cheap.

At some point, you must walk the talk.

WE ALL HAVE egos. Show me a business owner who doesn't have an ego!

Think about it.

At some point in that person's life, they had to make a conscious decision to think, *I can start something that someone out there is going to want to spend their money on.*

It's not arrogance.

It's confidence in your own ability to be good enough to make it happen.

Before my heart attack, I was at times blindly confident about some aspects of what I did. I could live any kind of lifestyle that I chose, and I could make it happen. That was the sporting competitor in me.

That was the 19-year-old who thought he was good enough to play midfield for the Ardboe senior team. When it came to setting up, running and organising a business, I had only one reference point.

I'd been to no business school.

I'd no degree… Masters, or PhD in business. I just knew what it took to run and organise a team. Gaelic football taught me that. I applied the lessons learned from being in the middle of changing rooms filled with successful men.

MY EXPERTISE IN growing a business in New York was rooted in the football fields and dressings-rooms of Ardboe and Tyrone teams. One hundred percent everything that I did, and do now, to grow Shoreline Builders Inc, is based on the same teamwork that it takes to develop a successful football team.

I know so many guys out in New York who will tell you exactly the same thing. Many of my friends here who own their own construction firms were and still are steeped in GAA, either at home or out here.

First rule. Only hire people that are better at the job than you are, and more intelligent than you. It can never all be about Mickey Coleman.

We would be closed if it was.

I wasn't intelligent enough to get my head around things like accounts receivable, accounts payable, income statements, and balance sheets. I learned all of that on the job from the people around me that walked and talked me through it.

Out on that first job, at the Cherokee Building on 77th Street, I had the mindset of building up the team.

In the early days I had no office.

I had a van. That was my office.

That was the only office that I needed for a while. The most overwhelming part of the expansion of Shoreline Builders was the day I rented an office in Yonkers, and then started to hire staff to work in it.

I'd ask myself the question.

If I was sitting in a dressing-room and about to go out onto the field... into the white-hot heat of a championship match, would I want that person I'm going to work with on my team?

Would he or she be good enough, or would he or she be on the subs' bench today?

That's how I viewed people.

That's how I measured the performance of people in my business.

Would I pass them the ball?

Would I be comfortable enough to know that they could kick a score for the team? Who could I trust to look after the business and makes the necessary interventions when needed?

I reverted to type.

This is my team. *How am I going to line them all out?*

Who would be responsible for all the different positions that I needed to fill? That's how I still run the business today.

WHEN I WALK into a board meeting with all my staff, I've got an accountant, a controller, director of operations and my purchasing guys.

My Director of Operations could build out a job with his eyes closed. I wouldn't know where to start at times. He's my centre-forward. He's the man driving things forward and dictating the pace of the scoring up front.

He helps me to deliver the promises made.

The inside forwards are the people in the field building and fitting out the jobs. My centre-back is definitely my accountant.

The full-back in the bank manager.

I work alongside the controller in midfield directing the traffic. I'm playing the balls in to get the best scores, but I'm also covering back the odd time. I sell the business. I get the business in. I can see more from *here*.

I can view all parts of the business from *here*.

I try to be hands-on.

Erin is the goalkeeper.

Nothing gets past her and that's the way it should be.

YOU'D THINK, BASED on the gaelic football comparison, that I'd be the manager of the team. Not really. I see myself in the position where I most comfortable. There is no point in me telling you that I know how to run all aspects of it, and that's why you need a good team around you.

When you are in there attempting to keep things going, there are a lot of moving parts. Change orders, purchase orders, budgets... it can be chaos at times and the pressure does come on. I see people in my office getting stressed about various projects.

That's why, for me, structure is important.

At times it isn't always about succeeding. But it's about being organised and structured in your approach. Since the widow-maker visited me, I have a clearer understanding of the need for a structure in most things that I do.

I'm still far from an expert or a big shot businessman.

I just know now how to break down the elements that go into running my business, and I'm a lot more content with how I do that these days than I was before.

My recovery from the heart attack forced me to think hard about how I go about keeping on top of things, without everything getting on *top* of me. Now I don't stress about the small things. Sure, sometimes someone will make a mistake and that mistake will hurt the business. But I try to look at it from a different vantage point these days.

Did we concede a goal because the person failed to try? Or because that person did their best to make the block and we conceded anyway?

In business, I believe that as long as you can look people in the eye, and say… 'I want to go out onto that field with you as my teammate'… you've always got a chance of succeeding.

So far so good.

We've avoided the machine guns.

PART **10**

Fix You

ANYONE FORTUNATE ENOUGH to survive a heart attack is given a huge reward.

Time.

Extra time.

With that time, comes clarity.

When you are lying there in the hospital bed, you've two options, make no mistake about it. It begins by feeling very sorry for yourself.

At the beginning, it can almost consume you. For some people that's the place that they remain in for the days, weeks… months, and years after the event.

There will come a period of time when you start thinking about how the hell you ended up here in the first place. The key to recovery is to make sure you embrace that feeling and do something positive about it.

That was the starting point for me.

I was desperate to understand how I ended up with three blocked arteries in the first place. As far as I was concerned, I was living a very healthy lifestyle. I was training almost every night.

I knew nothing about heart disease.

I knew nothing about what causes heart disease.

I just knew that I required a way back. The words that I use to type into the phone to source my research will live with me forever.

How do I reverse my heart disease?

Right from the beginning, a similar theme kept being displayed on the screen. Plant based nutrition. The drive to change my diet started almost immediately.

I'd thrown all my chips into the centre of the table.

I was all in.

It was this or nothing.

When you are in that position, there is no negotiating with yourself.

This had to happen. The only other option wasn't even an option. It was a dark road to the end. It was a fine line of getting out of where I was... or not.

MANY PEOPLE NEVER come out of that place.

Mentally, they never get it right.

Physically they appear to recover. Mentally they don't.

Search for the stories of any heart attack or cancer survivors, and you'll discover that the main issue that they have is their mental health.

What if this happens again?

'What if' consumes their lives.

'What if' can consume anyone's life.

Forget about that 'what if?' You've no time to contemplate it.

Time is too precious.

Oliver's letter said it all. *The tsunami has come.*

It has left a trail of destruction.

It's gone... You need to move on.

The transition to a plant-based diet wasn't something that came easy to me. In the early days of my recovery the hospital menu only offered me a mixture of meat and dairy products.

This confused me.

I'm attempting to recover from a huge heart attack and everything that I'm reading online suggests that I shouldn't even consider dairy and meat. And yet here it is... on the menu of the hospital that saved my life.

I was baffled by it. I still am.

At the beginning, Erin would have gone out to a couple of little vegan shops and carried me in food. She did this every day that I was in the hospital. Looking back on it all now, it feels like every little bit of vegan food that I ate was like me rebuilding my life like a jigsaw. Every meal represented another piece of the puzzle.

Today, I look at food as my medication.

Every time I eat a plant-based meal, I feel that it's healing me. Erin's sister, Nadine bought me a book around that time by an author called Caldwell

Esselstyn. He pioneered a programme to reverse heart disease. It boils down to excluding food like oil and nuts, and just consuming plant-based food.

I stuck to the diet strictly for almost 17 months.

We didn't cook with oil. We cooked with balsamic vinegar. It's really only since January 2023 that we started to ease up on this. It was hardcore stuff, and it was tough.

Really tough.

Every single morning, I'd eat three cups of spinach. It was boiled up, rinsed off, strained out, coated in balsamic vinegar, and covered with some nutritional yeast.

As Esselstyn points out, the lifejacket of the arteries is nitrous oxide. Nitrous oxide is big in the leafy greens… kale, cauliflower, and spinach.

When they are infused with balsamic vinegar it produces a reaction that gives off a lot of nitrous oxide. It's the difference between your arteries being like Teflon, rather than Velcro. I'd eat a half cup of oats in the form of porridge, with oat milk and a teaspoon of flaxseed, chia seed and a little bit of agave or maple syrup.

As time has gone on, I've dropped the guard a little bit, but I still haven't eaten any red meat.

My cheat these days is a little bit of fish.

The odd slice of pizza here and there, but those are few and far between. That makes it just a little bit easier, but for the most part it's all plant-based. As I work down in the city of Manhattan, I try and grab dinner in a vegan restaurant or at least somewhere that serves a vegan option.

Wholewheat pasta, vegetables, a fra diavolo, a red tomato sauce, snap peas and as much vegetables as I can. Sometimes, it's just rice and chickpeas. Perhaps even a little bit of salad and ezekiel bread.

Kidney beans, quinoa, couscous, tomatoes, onions, mushrooms, and peppers.

That's what I'd load into a plate these days.

AS I'M SITTING here writing this, I've just spotted a chocolate brownie perched on the island in the middle of my kitchen. I've no desire whatsoever to eat it.

Funny how the mind changes.

This all sounds very boring and it is very boring, but the results are great. My cholesterol has gone from 138 down to 28. My blood pressure has dropped to normal, my sugar levels are good, my triglyceride levelled out.

Everything just normalised.

When I started easing off on what I was eating, my cholesterol started to rise again. Everything that you eat is linked to it.

There is no question about that.

There's also a myth doing the rounds that all these athletes aren't getting enough protein to train. My diet is entirely plant-based, and I'm getting all the protein that I need. I'm training now as hard as I did before. Plants are providing me with what I need.

That, and three litres of water a day.

If you stick to the plan, the results will come, and they will come quickly.

Within a few weeks.

Unless you can potentially grow it in your backyard, forget about it.

THERE'S A SAYING in the part of the world that I come from… 'burning the candle at both ends'.

That's exactly what I was doing.

When you try to make a life in New York and set up a business here, you want to do everything in your power to make it work. That's all I wanted to do; make it work.

There's an expectation I guess that everyone places on themselves, that if you don't succeed in New York then you are a failure. No one else ever mentions it.

It's mainly inside your own head.

I am very driven when I put my mind to do most things. That can and sometimes does lead to stress. Anyone starting a business, knows exactly what the challenge is. You don't have the pay-roll, you don't have the capital that you need to buy materials to get up and running, and you certainly don't have the cashflow.

You are robbing Peter to pay Paul.

You are shaking and moving to make things work. You are borrowing money. You are putting money into the company and taking it back out again for something else. It's a s**t show. There are days when you just say to yourself that there must be an easier way to do this.

In the early days, I was building up massive debts hoping that things would turnaround quickly. Thankfully for me, they did. Today as a company, Shoreline is doing bigger stuff. That's great, but with it comes bigger problems.

The morning diet back then wasn't too pretty.

The pitstop on the way into the city often consisted of bacon, egg and cheese on a bagel. That was accompanied with a mandatory coffee with cream and sugar.

I never worried about diet because somewhere during the week I'd burn it all off on a run or a CrossFit session. Diet was always someone else's issue.

It was never mine. I wasn't putting on loads of weight, so everything was good. Inside, however, I'd no idea that my body was crying for help.

I was never a big steak or red meat person. I'd prefer chicken. I never thought twice about what I'd have for lunch or dinner. Never.

My stress levels were something different. I used to wake up in the morning and immediately start thinking about what I'd on that day. Maybe 20 different jobs on across the city. *Who owes me money today? Who do I owe money to today?*

Have I covered the insurance?

Every day I was running the gauntlet.

I bet that from the outside looking in, people who knew me might have thought… *Look at Mickey. He's going well. Look at how successful he has become.*

My life only consisted of reacting to situations. I wasn't in control. I thought I was in control… I wasn't.

It's no surprise looking back that I took a heart attack.

I was due one.

My way of dealing with it all was running. If I was running or in a CrossFit session, and I was thinking about work, I'd get it into my head that I wasn't training hard enough.

I'd train like a maniac.

Unless I was struggling to breathe, I wasn't training hard enough. I only realise now that this was my way of figuring out the stress.

When I first became consciously aware of what had happened to me, the initial thoughts were, *Where the hell am I going with all of this? How do I fix this?*

In the construction industry, things break.

They become decayed and unstable.

In the construction game, things can be fixed.

Surely, I can be fixed?

I SPENT MY time asking myself a series of questions that I really didn't have the answer to. Before you start answering these questions after a life-changing event like a heart attack, there are so many things that need to level out.

Your mental health feels like it's gone.

Your mind is in a spiral of torturous thoughts.

You are an emotional nightmare. Even to this day, I'm a much more emotional person than I ever was before. I did live in a world of the alpha male, and on hindsight it wasn't the greatest place to be. A world of needing to be tough, needing to be seen to be tough. It's all a load of s***e in my eyes now.

I'm happy enough to let my emotions take over now.

I have the odd weep to myself now and then. It's a release valve that I never turned to prior to my heart attack. I never cried in my adult life before, never felt that I could, never let my guard down.

It's not the done thing! I'd tell myself.

All that is just nonsense.

Complete and utter nonsense.

Cry if you have to cry.

It will make you feel better.

IN THOSE FIRST few days back in the house, I was intolerant of people around me. I must have been a torture for Erin, and my mother and sister, who were there to support me. My nerves were all over the place.

My mindset focused on the possibility of that raging pain returning to my chest. I was irritable. I could hardly sleep and, when I did, it was disrupted by thoughts of falling asleep and never wakening up again.

When you are trying to recover from an event like a heart attack, you've got so many things going on in your mind. You want to get back to where you were mentally. You physically want to get back to where you were too.

Your benchmark is always where you were *before*.

I've some news for you.

Forget that benchmark.

The tsunami has come and gone.

You are now a different person.

Set a different benchmark.

Set a better benchmark.

If it's the same one, then you are finished.

It's got to be a better benchmark than before.

I'm living proof that you can achieve it.

A VISIT FROM two friends of mine helped me to reassess just exactly how I could set new goals for my recovery. Rosemary Devlin is Fay's wife, whom I've mentioned earlier. As part of her recovery, Rosemary said she put great faith in the power of meditation.

Following that visit, I started to dive into researching it.

My meditation started with prayer. Praying the rosary. Erin's sister, Ned brought me in rosary beads in the hospital and I'd nothing else to do, so I just prayed. I'm no religious person let me assure you, but it's funny how you latch on to something that gives you peace of mind.

It would help me sleep.

I've now dedicated a space in my house where I do my meditation.

When I first tried meditation at home, I struggled with it. I just thought that it was a matter of closing my eyes and waiting for something magical to happen.

Then came a light bulb moment.

I was in the gym, and I forced myself to try meditating in the steam room after a workout. You really had to concentrate hard in the steam room, because it was so hot. I probably shouldn't have even been in a steam room, in the first place, with my condition.

Then I discovered Wayne Dwyer, who promotes a type of meditation called Japa.

Japa is an old Buddhist meditation which involves chanting. Most people will think I'm now mad in the head, but there are different forms of this, and Wayne breaks it down into simple terms.

It's a way of focusing yourself to reaffirm what you want to happen.

I'd repeat these lines quietly to myself.

I am healing.

I am well.

I am better.

It was never... I am getting better.

It was... I am better.

I REMEMBER OPENING my eyes after the meditation in the steam room, and realising that I'd been in there for almost 45 minutes. I couldn't believe it. It was then I realised that I could meditate properly.

When I got out of the gym, I rang Erin. 'You are not going to believe this, Erin... it's the real thing.

'It took me two months to get here, but I did it.'

From then on, I knew that I could get to that place. It was the closest feeling that I got to the 'out of body' that I experienced when I was unconscious in the hospital. Every time that I repeat a meditation, that's the type of feeling that I get.

It's almost like reconnecting with the source.

Whatever that *source* is.

That's the feeling.

The feeling of putting your brain in neutral. There will be some friends reading this who will joke, 'That's where Mickey's brain has been for most of his life'.

Yes, you get thoughts that pop into your head during meditation, but they are like cars passing by on a road. You don't fight those thoughts. You let them flow, you let them go.

You never really engage with them.

Through repetition, and through time, it becomes easier. The outside thoughts aren't ever as strong. It's important to find time to meditate every day, if you can. If you don't engage with it for a few days, there's a cluttering of the mind, with mostly negative and pressurised thoughts.

PULSE

I'M NOW IN a place where I need to meditate every day.

It's like a natural drug that keeps on giving.

It's like lifting a weight off your mind.

This is going to sound strange and a little bit mad, perhaps... but, you are wrapping yourself in a spiritual blanket.

You've a feeling like you are floating through the day, after it.

Unburdened by the heaviness that life throws at you.

Mentally cleansed... fulfilled.

These days, I go to a room upstairs in the house to meditate.

Sometimes I will have been on the phone to someone about work and I can start to feel the blood pressure rising, because I want to get into a physical fight to resolve it.

Then... I'm walking back down the stairs with a totally different perspective.

Everything is perspective, at the end of the day.

IN THE PAST, I would have been a very serious guy when it came to running my business. I'm not saying that anything has changed from that, as my staff could probably testify to, but I do try to reset when I can.

There's a difference is being really focused and uptight, and being focused properly. I have the drive to create a more successful business than the one that I run now. I still have ambition for my company. Clarity of mind makes that a lot easier now than it was prior to the widow-maker.

SIT ON THE edge of your bed and ask yourself a question.

Are you happy with your life?

If you aren't, work out what you are going to do to change it. If you are completely honest with yourself, you will get the answer that you need. It might not be the one that you want to hear, but I guarantee if you slow life down you will find the answer that you need.

There are loads of self-help people out there.

The internet and social media in particular are full of it. They want to help you increase your income. Increase your fitness levels. Turn you into the best person that you can be.

A person that everyone will want to be around.

Most of those ideas are what I would call '30 second plans'.

That's not going to help you.

I now do two things.

Two things that I've introduced into my life, and they really help me in any situation that I find myself in.

The first thing I do when I wake up every single morning is, I bless myself and I thank God that I opened my eyes. If you don't believe in the same God that I do, just thank someone.

Anyone.

The second thing I do is, I live in the present moment.

Every time.

I know better than anyone that nothing is guaranteed to us.

That's my way of bringing contentment and balance to my life now. You must create an inner peace and inner contentment within your own body to do anything. If you can create that, then you are on a good pathway. It's about quietening your mind and body.

No one creates the turmoil in your own head, only you.

Where am I tomorrow?

How will I get everything done that I need to get done?

How am I going to settle those bills?

Those aren't problems, if you live in the present moment.

Think about where you are right now.

Did you open your eyes this morning?

A lot of people didn't.

You will find a way through the clutter. Don't walk out through the door with a load of obstacles in your way. You will never achieve anything if you do.

Are you breathing?

Have you got someone that cares about you?

I bet that you are in a much better place than you think you are. Ninety-five percent of the things that you worry about, never come true.

I always bring it back to that.

Every single time that I get into a tough situation in work, that's what I do. I don't get uptight anymore. I don't let things get out of control.

Play your music.

Everyone has music to play... *inside.*

Don't reach your death bed never having played your music.

'Anything is Possible'
'You've got to dream like you've never seen obstacles'
'Thrive, Prosper, Aspire'

(Quotes on the wall of the Montefiore Nyack Hospital
Cardiac Rehab Centre where I did my rehab sessions)

THE BUILDING BLOCKS for a return from illness, in my opinion, begin with stripping yourself bare of who you were.

The starting point is emotional cleansing.

You must ask yourself the hard questions.

You really need to be honest with yourself. I would never have been a person that was able to express myself emotionally.

I was the alpha male.

I was living with the hard man façade all around me.

It was a load of nonsense.

I was a bluffer.

Some would say I still am. I can have the craic, but I'm honestly not bluffing the most important person in the room anymore. Myself.

You can't cheat the person in the mirror. You can make all of the excuses that you want, but you can't tell lies to the person staring back at you in the mirror. After 41 years of living on this earth, I found that it took the biggest life changing event of my life to let me know who I really was.

I WAS ON my knees. I knew that I had to rebuild. I knew that I couldn't rebuild as the old Mickey. The sign of insanity if continuing to do the same things you've always done and expecting different results.

If you do what you always do, you will always get what you always got.

I live every day based on attempting to do the right thing. If I've got it in my head that I might want to do something with the two kids today, I just go ahead and do it. It's not always going to be this way.

For 10 years in this country (United States of America) I chased money. The money always seemed to run faster than me. Money is a by-product of your happiness and your contentment. If you are content in yourself, you have peace in yourself. Money isn't wealth to me. You need to get your mindset around that.

We are socially programmed to worry about the amount of money in our bank account or the type of car that we are driving. I work in New York City five days a week. New York is an extreme place. No one has time to talk.

Sometimes, I take the train into work. Everybody is on their phone. Work for them begins a long time before they hit the office. Answering emails on phones and laptops. People stressed to the eyeballs. Some people working three jobs a week.

Would you see that as a normal way of living life?

IT'S MADNESS, TO live through your working life and to look back when you retire… to what? You chased your whole life to get to where you are at. How much of that time did you live? I mean *really* live.

We all look at this world through a different lens. Your view of it will be different from mine. The view of your friends different again.

I can't get this point across strong enough. You need to STOP!

Hit the bloody reset button and hit it hard.

Do I love me? Am I really doing what is best for me?

This is going to sound harsh. Forget about your kids, your partner, and your friends. Ask yourself the question.

Am I in the place where I need to be?

Are the people around me really getting the best version of me?

I can assure you this much, when I woke up after coming out of a coma for three days, I would have emptied the bank account to have the energy to hug my two boys again.

Everything that I'd focused my attention on for 10 years in this country was f***ing useless to me when I needed it. It's easy for me to share that with you, because I've been where I've been.

For people who haven't been in that situation, it's very hard for them to get their head around it. If something in your life doesn't feel like it's ticking the box for you, then you need to sit on the edge of your bed and ask yourself the question.

How do I change this?

TO FIX WHAT'S going on around you, start by fixing what's going on inside you. That will take care of everything else. Anything is possible. You've got to dream like you've never seen obstacles.

Thrive... Prosper... Aspire.

When you can, drop the façade and sometimes admit that you aren't in control of everything. And stop pretending that you are. Stop living up to the expectations of other people and simply be realistic about your limitations; that will change your life.

That's going to change your decision making and make such a difference to the way that people interact with you. Watch the difference it makes. It will bring so many good people into your life.

In the past, I'd have brushed people aside because my focus was elsewhere.

I haven't mastered it yet, but now I stop and consciously try and work out who the human being in front of me actually is. They aren't just a name, and skin and flesh. They've got their worries, their hopes, their aspirations, and their own view of the world that they carry around with them every day.

You can't step into their shoes and live for them, but you can take time to acknowledge the fact that their lens is different from yours.

Some people have the right perspective already but from what I can see, the vast majority of people don't. Life changing events like a heart attack alter your perspective. You don't have to experience a heart attack to get focused in on the right perspective.

Believe me. There are easier ways to reset your priorities than waiting until you recover from a widow maker.

That might not be an option for you.

Play your Music

When you try your best, but you don't succeed
When you get what you want, but not what you need
When you feel so tired, but you can't sleep
Stuck in reverse

And the tears come streaming down your face
When you lose something, you can't replace
When you love someone, but it goes to waste
Could it be worse?

Lights will guide you home
And ignite your bones
And I will try to fix you

(*Fix You* by Coldplay)

I'M IN THE privileged position of knowing the outcome of a build-up of pressure and living the wrong type of lifestyle, and being able to provide you with the full commentary on it.

I don't want to be seen as some kind of evangelist in all of this, but people have asked me many times since that day if it has changed me as a person?

There are those that think that they know what it takes to return from where I've been. Those people are singing from the gallery.

Unless you've been there, then forget about it.

I've been in the arena when the fight was on.

I've been in the middle of the fight.

Being on the wrong side of your mental capacity to cope with the simple acts of just breathing, moving your arms and legs, talking to the people that you love is an incredibly tough place to be.

I would never want anyone to ever be there.

Ever.

IT'S NOT A great place to come back from, and some people don't come back from it very well. The scars are deep and they hang around.

But there is hope.

I'm living proof of that.

There is so much to be grateful for. There are days that I'm sitting in my office, and I almost have to pinch myself.

How did I end up here?

How lucky am I to be alive and to have people around me that I love.

In my mind, if you want to make it in this world, you need to show respect for the people around you. Whether you are the CEO of a company or the guy who's out on a building site labouring to a bricklayer, you need to see the value of the people around you.

Being able to listen to someone, and being able to share and take advice from them, and being grateful for that advice, only makes you a better person. I marvel at and respect the people around me that bring a sense of calmness and warmth to the way they interact with others.

They bring such a lovely energy to any given situation.

That's the type of person that I'm striving to be.

Perspective in business and in life.

Is anybody dead? No.

Is anyone injured? No.

Then we can figure everything else out from here.

It's not that big of a deal.

It's all good.

IN SHORELINE, I'VE implemented a solution-based attitude to the many obstacles that we cross during the working day. Don't bring a problem to anyone unless you've at least one suggestion for a solution. I've witnessed how that can positively change the whole dynamic in a room.

The power of recovery from the widow-maker has provided me with a clarity of insight into situations that I've never had before.

I knew that I had to believe that I was going to get better.

Believe it.

Be it.

I had to convince myself of that.

Your mind is a very powerful thing. From time to time, I would get flutters of sudden movements in my heart and I'd smile and tell myself that this was my heart finding a way to heal.

'I am healing. I am getting better.'

I'd lock out any negative thoughts. As I mentioned before, meditation helped me to achieve that. If I've a message for you, it's that you have to invest in yourself. When you do that and truly believe that your mind will help change your well-being, it's the most powerful thing that you can discover.

I am well.

I am getting stronger.

I feel better.

That's the secret to it. When you tell yourself this, you actually do begin to feel better. That's what happened me. I reversed my heart disease.

I'm also so conscious of the fact that some people reading this might well know someone who has or is suffering from a terminal disease where no recovery is possible.

I'm not playing the hand of God in this.

All I can say is that you should tell yourself that you are getting better. Tell yourself that every chance that you get during the day. That will create a better vibe and feeling within you. If you don't get better, then you will have lived your life to the end in a much better state of mind, and inspired those that you love and leave behind.

I WILL BE honest.

When I started out on this journey of recovery, I had no idea of whether or not I would make a full recovery.

I could so easily have gone the other way. I still could.

Whether I was getting better or not, I was feeling better. My thought process was positive. I'm no whacky religious freak when I tell you that there is a divine energy and intelligence around us all. We all need to pay attention to it.

When you are where I was, you need to pay attention to it. When you are as sick as I was, you will be looking for answers. Don't wait until then to discover it.

When you discover it, you will feel energised.

Ask yourself a question.

What's the one thing that makes your heart beat?

What makes your hair grow, or not in some cases?

What makes your fingernails grow?

There's an energy all around us, and in us.

Do we really pay attention to it?

Trees grow, flowers will blossom, and the rivers will run. The world works exactly how it is supposed to work. The world works exactly how it's meant to work.

I have thought so much about the whole 'out of body' experience that I have had. No brain surgeon can open my head, find the right part of my brain... and point to the part of my head that made me feel like that.

If they could, they would box it and sell it. It doesn't actually exist in the physical world. Where is that thought? You can't touch and you can't see it. That's the spiritual dimension. The key now is to transfer that into the physical domain.

The house that I'm sitting in today was once a thought by someone, at one time, that's been transferred into a physical manifestation of that thought. Where is that thought now?

We aren't human beings having a spiritual experience.

We are spiritual beings having a human experience.

You might not believe this, but I can assure you that you are in complete control of every aspect of your life, thought-wise.

Can you imagine waking up every single day of your life having that tremendously positive feeling that all is well in the world. You would live your life in a completely different way.

What's stopping you?

It's only a thought process.

Search for it.

Get that feeling in your belly.

Love beats everything.

When that takes over, everything else dissolves.

That begins as a thought process.

Wayne Dwyer describes it brilliantly. When you take an orange, and you squeeze it, what comes out of that orange is 100% of what is inside it.

What is inside you?

Pressures, anxiety, hatred in your heart?

You create that. I was that person. Every day of my life before the widow-maker that's who I was. The environment that I was living in… I created it. I'd no one to blame only myself. I was a product of who I was.

A complete product of my choices.

THERE'S NO ONE going through this world without some element of pain. If they are, then they are going to experience it at some point in their life.

For those of you cringing and laughing at some of what I've written in this book, some day you will be asking for advice on how to cope. Maybe not from me, but from someone else.

How do I know that?

Because I was that guy.

Don't let your circumstances define you. Don't blame anyone else.

Sit on the edge of your bed and ask yourself the hard questions. When I did that, I cried like a child. In my bedroom at the top of the stairs.

The same set of stairs, at the bottom of which I almost died.

IT BREAKS MY heart even now thinking about the torment that I put people through during those days in hospital. It couldn't have happened at a worse time for my family back in Ardboe.

The world was still in the midst of dealing with a global Covid 19 pandemic and my parents, and my brothers and sisters at home couldn't come out to see me. They relied solely upon Erin face-timing them from my bedside. What must have been going through their heads watching me being kept alive by tubes and machines.

Three and a half thousand miles away.

Watching their son and brother fighting for his life.

It's overwhelming at times.

I guess for them as well there was also the thought process as to whether they were getting all of the right information, or were they being protected from some of it?

And high up above, or down below
When you're too in love to let it go
But if you never try, you'll never know
Just what you're worth

AND THEN, THERE was Erin.

How did she juggle all of those emotions?

Her own emotions and her own heartache of sitting there wondering what the future would hold for her and our two beautiful boys? It was a monumental act of strength from her. She comes from good stock in being part Tyrone part Kerry, but in all seriousness there really aren't any words to credit her properly with how she handled everything.

How she continues to handle everything.

The doctors didn't fill anyone with much hope in those early minutes and hours. Not too many people play with a 6% chance of survival and live to tell the tale.

Recovery was never going to be simple.

If recovery was possible at all? The prognosis wasn't great. Yes, the doctors had mended the left anterior descending artery but in the aftermath of me wakening up from the coma, they told me that they'd more work to do.

The emergency stent was doing its job but I required two more stents shortly, as I had 95% blockages in another two arteries. The procedure to insert those wouldn't take place until I well enough to go through the operation.

I remember when he told me that.

All I was thinking at the time was… *Is that not something you need to be getting on with now?*

Right now!

The team that looked after me were phenomenal. Absolutely amazing. They never took a single incorrect step in helping to secure my future. All the goodwill and the prayers for me gave me the energy to turn it all around. I'd lay there in the stillness of that hospital bed, and I'd think that I needed to make the next day, a better day than this one.

Deep down in my heart and soul I knew that physically I would make it back.

I knew that prior to that fateful day I was strong, and physically fit to handle what I went through. Mentally I was at rock bottom. I'd a big mountain to climb, but I was prepared to do it.

The bottom line is that when your back is against the wall, you have nothing only your own strength to allow you inhale the air around you... and breathe. Rarely will anyone ever experience that type of feeling.

The human spirit's will to live is a very powerful thing.

When I learned to accept it, I became enclosed in a spiritual blanket that had been thrown over me. That fed me with the energy that I needed, to convince myself that I was going to get better.

It's difficult, I realise, to convince others that I'm not just a little bit crazy when they hear me talking like that. The spiritual realm isn't something that people are convinced about. It's always *someone else* that might experience it.

People who pass away experience it.

I know that to be true.

I spent 10 years of my life in America chasing the dream. Chasing the glory of money and big houses and cars, and all of that kind of stuff. For the most part, it happened.

I achieved some of it.

Illness, of course, remains the greatest leveller.

All those materialistic pressures are all for nothing when you lie there hoping that your next breath won't be your last. There's a saying that a man wants a million things, and a sick man wants just one thing.

I can testify to that.

You run a race and you can have all the support in the world during that race. You should run it to the best of your ability, but you need to realise that it's your race. Your own race. It's up to you how you reach the finish line.

That Coldplay song *Fix You* came on the radio one morning when I was using the small gym that I'd built for myself at the house. When I heard it, I turned it up and stopped what I was doing.

> *Tears stream down your face*
> *I promise you I will learn from my mistakes*
> *Tears stream down your face, and I*
>
> *Lights will guide you home*
> *And ignite your bones*
> *And I will try to fix you*

I STARTED TO cry.

Flood and floods of tears. But they were different this time.

I wasn't sad.

I'd achieved something.

I'd fixed myself to the point that I was able to train again… and train hard.

A huge milestone.

I'd done the job.

The alpha male had disappeared.

I was at peace with myself.

If I were offered the chance now to go back to March 29, 2021 and stop the widow-maker, I wouldn't stop it. I wouldn't change a thing.

I occupy a different world now. It's not physically different but my mindset now presents it to me in a very different light.

I live life to the beat of a new rhythm.

MY ADVICE TO you is simple.

Live in the present moment, because I almost left this world without playing my music.

Play your music.

Listen to me… *Play your music.*

Because your life can change in a heartbeat.

Mine did.

Mickey Coleman and his wife, Erin and their sons,
Micháel and Riordan in 2023